SCIENCE SORTED

Robots, chips and techno stuff

By Glenn Murphy

Illustrated by Mike Phillips

MACMILLAN CHILDREN'S BOOKS

This book is produced in association with the Science Museum. Royalties from the sale of this product help fund the museum's exhibitions and programmes.

Internationally recognized as one of the world's leading science centres, the Science Museum, London, contains more than 10,000 amazing exhibits, two fantastic simulator rides and the astounding IMAX cinema. Enter a world of discovery and achievement, where you can see, touch and experience real objects and icons which have shaped the world we live in today or visit **www.sciencemuseum.org.uk** to find out more.

First published 2011 by Macmillan Children's Books
a division of Macmillan Publishers Limited
20 New Wharf Road, London N1 9RR
Basingstoke and Oxford
Associated companies throughout the world
www.panmacmillan.com

ISBN 978-0-330-50896-4

1 3 5 7 9 8 6 4 2

A CIP catalogue record for this book is available from the British Library.

Typeset by Nigel Hazle
Printed and bound in the UK by CPI Mackays, Chatham ME5 8TD

Thanks to:

Gaby Morgan, Dominic Kingston, Lauren Ace and all at Macmillan Children's Books who continue to offer their help and support.

Wendy Burford, Dan Albert and Charlotte Connelly at the Science Museum, London, and Tom Woolley at the National Media Museum – thanks for setting me straight as I ambled into unfamiliar techno-territory. Your comments and suggestions were all much appreciated. Thanks also to Mark Steed for keeping calm under fire and handling the last-minute Science Museum events with aplomb. Cheers, man!

Dr Eddie Grant and Dr Min Ki Lee of the North Carolina State University Centre for Robotics and Intelligent Machines – I hugely enjoyed talking with you both, and your insights and predictions for the future of robotics made this book at least twice as interesting as it would have been.

Jennifer Weston at NCSU for making the above conversations possible!

Michael C. Harris of Rockwell Automation – your descriptions of industrial robots and the basics of robot movement and programming were a big help – thanks so much for taking the time to chat.

Jeff Shearer, also of Rockwell Automation, for helping with the above and for being an all-round top bloke.

Jimmy Lee at Innvo Labs for sending me my very own Pleo!

Henry Walker and all the staff and pupils of the Carolina Friends School. Once again you were an inspiration to me in finishing this book.

Helen (Crewella) and Belle for Pleo-rescue services above and beyond the call of duty. Was great to meet you both!

As always, to the Murphs, the Witts and all our family and friends . . .

. . . and to Heather, Ka-ge and Austin – it's nice to go away, but it's so much nicer to come home.

Contents

Introduction – The Digital World

When my parents were growing up, robots and computers were the stuff of science fiction. They were things people read about in storybooks, or saw clunking and bleeping away in science-fiction movies. Back then, if you were lucky enough to own a television or telephone, it was heavy, awkward and tethered to your house. Music was either played live by musicians, or played at home on a scratchy record player. In your wildest dreams, you could never have imagined things like laptops, mp3 players, smartphones or portable DVD players.

So what? I mean, that was probably *ages* ago, right?

Not really, no. Here are a few things that happened *ages* ago:*

AD 43	Invasion of Britain by the Romans
1066	Invasion of Britain by William the Conqueror
1492	Christopher Columbus 'discovers' America

* Some of which you may already know about, if you've read the other Science Sorted books (hint, hint!).

1610	Galileo spots the moons of Jupiter with his telescope
1859	Charles Darwin describes his theory of evolution

My parents were born in the mid-twentieth century, just **sixty years** or so before you. This might *seem* like a long time, but, if you think about it, it really isn't. Not when you realize that within that short time **the entire world has changed**.

Today, robots build our cars, computers control our aeroplanes and, at any one time, millions of people are chatting wirelessly through mobile phones and internet connections. Today, my mum emails her friends daily from her laptop. And my dad . . . well . . . he fiddles with the DVD player until he gets it to work.

Yeah, yeah, yeah. Old people didn't have robots or computers, and now we do. That's all *amazing* and all that. But *so what*? I mean, what's the big deal?

What's the big deal? The big deal is that you live in an incredible, super-charged, super-connected digital world that your grandparents could never have dreamed of. But do you know how it all *works*?

Course I do. You just switch on the computer, click the 'email' thingy, and . . .

Okay, so maybe you know how to *use* computers, but do you know how to *fix* one or *build* one? If someone asked you to, could you design a robot, a smartphone or a 3DTV?

Well, if you put it that way . . . err . . . no. I s'pose not.

Here are some even simpler ones for you: *what is* a robot? And *what is* a computer?

Easy! A robot is like a big, metal . . . err . . . person, and a computer's like an electronic box with . . . well . . . you type on it, and there's a mouse and windows and stuff, and . . . (sigh). Maybe it's not that easy after all.

Wouldn't you like to know the answers to those questions?

I bought this book, didn't I?

Good point.

Go on, then.

Right – first up: **robots**.

In short, a **robot** is a machine that **does things for humans**. Usually boring, difficult or dangerous **work** that humans *could* do, but really rather wouldn't. The word *robot* actually comes from the Czech word *robota*, meaning 'worker' or 'slave'. So robots are basically electromechanical slaves built to serve their human masters. *Some* robots look like humans, or mimic human movements. But many don't. Most robots look nothing like humans, and move more like snakes, insects or other animals.

Really? Robot snakes and insects?

Yep – more about those later. For now, it's enough to know this: right now, there are *millions* of robots in the world, doing *millions* of tough, tricky jobs – on land, on sea, underground and even underwater. And to *build* a working robot, motors, batteries and body parts are not enough. You also need to give it some sort of electronic brain or controller. That's where **computers** come in.

Okay, then – so what's a computer, and how do you build one of those?

A computer is any device that helps humans to deal with (or make sense of) information. They get their name from the word *compute*, which means *to add up*. This is because the earliest computers were simple counting tools, used to do sums that were too tricky for humans to do easily in their heads. Over time, these developed into modern computers, which are electronic machines that not only help us make sense of numbers, but also of patterns, pictures, words, chess moves and much, much more.

Basically, computers *take in information* (or **input**), *work* with it (or **process** it) and then *churn it out* again in a more useful form, as **output**. In the very simplest computers, that's pretty much the end of the story. In more complex computers, the **output** becomes another **input**, and the information goes through the **input-output** cycle thousands and thousands of times before the final output pops out. But the idea is pretty much the same. Computers **process inputs into useful outputs.** That's it.

Now to build a computer, you obviously need *things to input with* (like a **keyboard** or a **mouse**), *things to output with* (like a **monitor** or **printer**) and *things to store and process information with* (like **memory banks**, **storage drives** and a **Central Processing Unit**). Together, all this stuff is known as ***hardware***. Bits of computer hardware can differ in shape, size and power, but they all work in more or less the same way. A keyboard has keys, and you type on it. A monitor has a screen, which lights up to display information. A printer sprays ink on to paper to copy out screen information, and so on.

But if all computers are built more or less the same way, then how do you get them to do so many different types of things?

Ahh, good question. That's all down to ***software***. Computer software is a program or set of instructions that tells a computer what to do. Without software, a computer is just a heap of useless (but rather expensive) junk. By creating different types of software, and using it to **program** computer hardware in different ways, you can turn a simple number-crunching machine into a handy, multipurpose tool. One you can use for everything from emailing and instant-messaging to predicting the weather and searching the skies for signs of alien life.

Computers really do all that?

Yep. All that and more. Not only that, computers are still developing at an incredible rate. They're getting smaller, faster and more powerful every year. They're supercharging our radios, TVs, mp3 players and smartphones, building whole new worlds through the Internet, and leading to a whole new generation of intelligent robots and androids. This is the amazing digital world we'll be exploring in this book.

We'll find out how computers 'think', and meet the world's largest and tiniest computers. We'll see how computers control our gadgets, and peek into **the future of televisions, mp3 players, mobile phones** and **video games**. We'll discover how the **Internet** works, and how it could change future schools and lessons. And, finally, we'll explore the wide world of **robots**. We'll meet **huge robots, tiny robots, pet robots, battle robots** and **humanlike androids** that walk, talk and act just like real people.

Whoa! Sounds like quite a ride. So where do we start?

With the birth of the computer, and the rise of thinking machines . . .

1. Thinking Machines

Are computers just posh calculators?

The first ones were, yes. The earliest computers were huge, complex, mechanical counting machines, fit for little more than doing complex sums. But from the 1970s onwards engineers developed them into something completely different – powerful, multipurpose machines that would rule the world.

What?! Computers rule the world?!!! Nobody told me!!! Aghhhhhhh!!! Run for your lives!!!!

Whoa, there. Calm down. I didn't mean that computers literally rule the world – like kings, queens or presidents. I meant that in the twenty-first century, computers control everything from car engines to spy satellites, from hospital visits to criminal records, from bank transfers to air-traffic control. But thankfully there are still actual people in charge of programming and operating them. For now at least, human drivers are still driving our cars, human bankers and shoppers make our money transfers, and human pilots and air-traffic controllers fly and land our aeroplanes.

Ohh. I see. Well, that's a relief. For a minute there, I thought we were done for. So computers

control the world, but we still control computers?
Something like that, yes.

So what were the first computers like?
For the most part, they were big, clunky and very, very limited in what they could do.

In a way, the earliest 'computer' (or computing device) was the abacus. This primitive number-cruncher dates back to around 2500 BC, and was used by the mathematicians of ancient Babylonia (who lived in what is now known as Iraq).

Why there?
Because that's where large-scale farming (and towns and cities supported by farming) first developed. Before farming and civilization, there was little need to keep track of large numbers, and people rarely needed to add up to numbers higher than they could count on their fingers.* But that all changed once farmers started trading seeds, crops and livestock. So the abacus was invented to help calculate trades between farmers, merchants and customers. Later, Chinese mathematicians and craftsmen made handy, portable abacuses using beads threaded on to wire. And for the next 4,000 years or so, people made do with these primitive 'computers' just fine. But by the

---

* In the languages of some Indonesian hunting tribes, there aren't even words for numbers greater than three. Some of these tribes still count like this today: 'one . . . two . . . three . . . many'.

seventeenth century, life in some parts of the world had become a lot more hectic. In Europe, science and engineering were starting to take off in a big way, and scientists, engineers and mathematicians needed new ways to calculate larger numbers. In 1642, French mathematician Blaise Pascal invented the first mechanical calculator, which cranked out eight-digit additions using hand-turned cogs, gears and wheels. But, amazing as it was, Pascal's machine couldn't subtract, multiply or divide – only add – so it was still a long way from the digital calculators and computers of today.

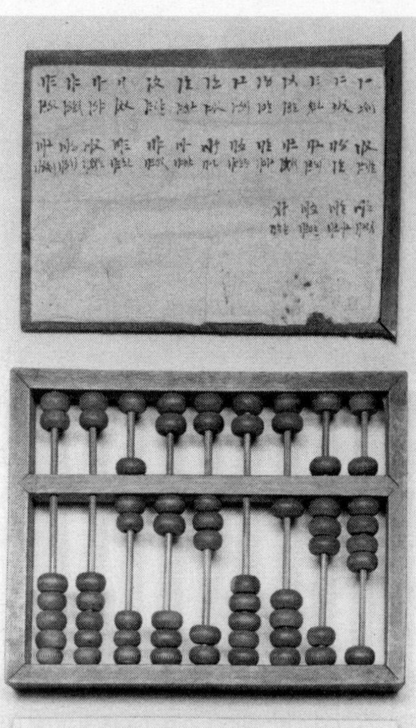

In 1849, English inventor Charles Babbage went one better, and designed his enormously complex 'difference engine'. Babbage never lived to see his designs become reality, but when the Science Museum built the machine according to his original plans it was made up of 25,000 individual parts.

It could perform complex multiplication sums up to thirty decimal places and had many of the basic elements of modern computers, including a memory, a processor and switchable functions or programs.

But, nifty as it was, it was still basically just a big, mechanical adding-machine. The world had to wait another 100 years before the first multipurpose computers (i.e. machines that could do more than just big sums) came along.

Why that long?

Well, it took that long for complex **electronics** to develop. While Pascal and Babbage's 'computers' were based on **mechanical gears and switches**, modern computers are based on **electronic circuits and switches.**

Basically, no matter how cleverly it's designed, there's only so fast you can go with a hand-operated, all-mechanical computer. The (human) operator turns a crank, the gears whirr and grind together, mechanical switches are flipped and eventually the solution to your problem is clicked out. You can try to speed things up by turning the wheels faster, but there's only so fast you can turn the wheels before a) the gears wear out, or b) your arm wears out. Now compare that with electronic circuits, which don't move at all. Instead, information is transferred via electricity, which can whip through hundreds (even thousands) of electronic switches per second.

So once you have those you can build a desktop or a laptop?

Errr . . . not quite, no. The valves and switches that went into the first electronic computers were much bigger than the microscopic circuits we use today. This made the computers themselves pretty chunky as a result.

Chunky? Like, how chunky? Bigger than a washing machine?

Bigger.

Bigger than a fridge-freezer?

Yep. Bigger than your kitchen, probably. One of the first successful electronic computers, UNIVAC, filled an entire room with its super-sized circuits, fans and magnetic memory drums.

Yikes!

Exactly. It wasn't until the invention of microchips – thin wafers of silicon* stamped with tiny electronic circuits – that more powerful (and less massive!) computers became possible. The first computers with microprocessors were built in the 1970s, and the first personal computers (or desktop PCs) arrived shortly afterwards. From that point on, computers began to double in processing power every couple of years. And, within a few decades, the first, boxy PCs turned into laptops, palmtops, tablet computers and more.

Good thing too.

How's that?

Well, it'd be a bit tricky checking your email with a fridge-sized laptop on your knees . . .

---

* For this reason, people used to call them 'silicon chips'. So if you hear older folks saying this that's why.

Techno-facts: Early Computers

Think your home computer is a bit clunky, and could use more memory and power? Then check out these bad boys. In their time, these computers were about the smallest and best you could get. Good thing they've come on a bit . . .

Computer	Year	Memory*	Weight	Size of a . . .
UNIVAC	1951	1–9kB	24,000 kg (53,000 lb)	Room
Altair 8800	1975	32–64kB	13 kg (30 lb)	Suitcase
Apple Macintosh	1984	128kB	7 kg (16 lb)	Beach ball
Apple Powerbook	1993	160MB	3 kg (7 lb)	Cushion
Apple Macbook Air	2010	256GB	1 kg (2.2 lb)	Notepad

* Computer memory is measured in the number of **bytes** of information it can hold. A **byte** is equal to eight bits of digital information. For bigger memory banks a **Kilobyte (KB)** is a **thousand** bytes, a **Megabyte (MB)** is a **million** bytes and a **Gigabyte (GB)** is a **trillion** bytes.

Do computers eat microchips?

Computers don't eat microchips, but you will find them in the belly of every computer in the world. A microchip isn't a tasty digital snack. It's a miniaturized electronic circuit that forms the core of all modern computers, gaming consoles, e-readers, mobile phones and mp3 players. Without microchips, our modern, computerized world would not exist.

Really? They're that important to computers?

Yep. They're that important. In many ways, microchips *are* computers. Everything else is just there to help them do their job.

So what are they, exactly?

Microchips (also known as **integrated circuits, ICs**, or simply '**chips**') are miniaturized electronic circuits, first invented by US Army engineer Jack Kilby* in 1958. They're made taking a thin slice of semiconducting** material (Kilby's original chip used germanium, but most modern ones are made from silicon), then adding thin tracks and layers of metals to create tiny electrical components such

---

* Later, in the year 2000, he won a Nobel Prize in Physics for his invention. I guess it took the judges forty-two years to figure out that the microchip was a rather clever idea.

** Semiconductors are materials that conduct electricity in a special way. **Conductors** allow electricity to flow freely through them. **Insulators** do not. **Semiconductors** are somewhere in between.

as **transistors**, **capacitors** and **resistors**. A single microchip may contain millions (or even **billions**) of these components, yet they rarely measure more than a few centimetres across. In fact, the smallest ones around today measure less than a **thousandth of a millimetre** across. If you were bored (or crazy) enough to try, you could place over **4,000** of them, side by side, on the head of a single pin!

But what are all those electrical bits and pieces for, and why do we have to make them so tiny? Computers are basically just big collections of electrical switches, which interact to calculate certain outputs from inputs (we'll find out more about how this works later on). As we've already learned, the earliest calculators and computers had mechanical switches. But from the mid-twentieth century onward, they were built with electrical switches (or **transistors**) instead. With a few transistors connected in an electrical circuit, you have enough switches to create a simple calculator, which can add, subtract and do other simple sums. With a few hundred transistors, you can create a very simple computer, capable of doing complex sums like multiplying, dividing and finding square roots, correct to ten or more decimal places. With a few billion transistors, you can build a highly sophisticated computer like the PCs, laptops and tablets you see around you today.

But before the microchip came along engineers had a major problem. Early electrical transistors (at least the ones built before the 1970s) weren't that tiny. The early ones were about the same size as a matchbox. So sticking even a few hundred of them together built a chunky computer roughly the size of a sofa. With a few thousand transistors, your computer would fill an entire room. So a few billion? Forget it.

Microchips solved the size problem for computers. By etching thousands or millions of transistors on to a single chip, powerful computers could be made in more manageable sizes. This not only made the small desktop personal computer possible, it also allowed miniature computerized controllers to be built into everything from cars to mp3 players, from car engines to e-readers, and from Wiis to 3DTVs.

Is that all you need to build a computer, then? Just one microchip?
Well, the microchip is the *core* of the computer, yes. Every computer is built around one or more microprocessor, which function as the computer's Central Processing Unit (or CPU). But to build a fully functional, usable home computer, you need a few more things. You need some sort of **memory**, through which the CPU can store and retrieve information. You need an **input device**, like a keyboard, mouse or touchpad. You need an **output** (or **display**) **device**, like a monitor or printer. And, of course, you need a **power supply**, with which to provide the whole lot with electricity.

So if you had all those things, and you wired them to a single microchip, you'd have a proper, working computer?
Pretty much, yes.

So why do computers come in big boxes or cases, then? I mean, even laptops are . . . well . . . lap-sized.
That's mostly for convenience – to keep all the bits safely and tidily together in one place. I mean you could just leave your expensive microchip out on the table, and have wires trailing everywhere connecting it to your monitor, keyboard and such. But you probably wouldn't be too happy if your cat ate it, or

your little sister spilled juice over the whole lot. Plus, there are a few more things in the 'box' that help keep the computer running smoothly. If you were to open up an average home computer, here's what you'd find inside:

Motherboard – a big, printed circuit-board about the size of an A4 sketch pad. This provides a handy base for most of the computer's essential parts, along with connectors for input and output devices like monitors and keyboards.

CPU – the microprocessor that forms the core of the computer. This sits within a little frame on the motherboard, usually with a small, box-like fan on top. Microchips heat up quite a bit as they work, so the fan is needed to keep them from overheating.

RAM – the RAM (random access memory) – another chip on the motherboard, which stores information temporarily while the computer is running. This type of memory has no moving parts, so can transfer information very quickly. But it is erased every time you switch your computer off.

Hard-disk drive (or **HDD**) – your computer's permanent memory bank. This contains the computer's operating system program (e.g. Windows) along with all other programs, text documents, pictures, video files and music files. It sits in its own box, separate from the motherboard and looks like a miniature CD player – with a small, spinning disc in the middle which is scanned rapidly by a little moving arm. When it's running, the disc rotates at over 7,000 revolutions per minute, and the arm moves so quickly it's little more than a blur.

Optical drive – most (but not all) computers have CD, DVD or Blu-Ray drives for loading software, playing music, movies and games, and saving information on to disk. Disk drives sit in their own little box (with the disk tray or slot sticking out of the computer casing), connected to the motherboard by cables.

Power supply – a power transformer which supplies power to all electrical devices inside the computer. In a PC, this is a little box *inside* the computer casing, connected to the motherboard, drives and other parts by wires. In a laptop, the box sits outside the main computer, and is used to recharge the **battery**.

Fans – fans inside the computer casing keep the warm air generated inside moving through, which keeps components cool and prevents damage from overheating.

Case – this is just a big box (usually plastic, but it can be made of anything from aluminium to bamboo) that surrounds the computer's components. It contains everything we've already mentioned.

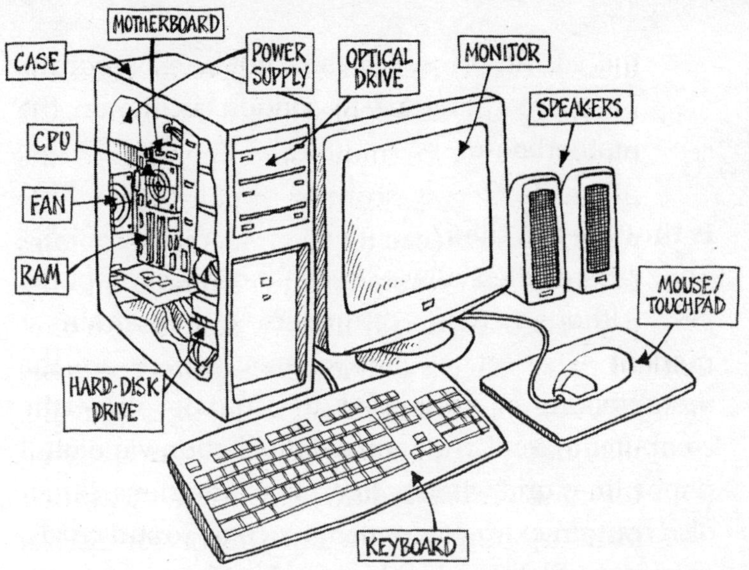

Keyboard – used to input characters and program the computer. Attaches to the motherboard via a cable in most PCs, but some are connected by wireless (Bluetooth or infrared) transmitters and receivers. In a laptop, the keyboard sits right on top of the motherboard.*

Monitor – output device used to display characters, images and video onscreen. Attaches to the casing and motherboard via cables.

Mouse/touchpad – input devices used to control onscreen cursors, select icons and scroll text.

Speakers – amplify sounds, music and video audio tracks. In a laptop, these may be built into

* For this reason, spilling water or juice over your laptop may destroy the whole computer, whereas spilling it over a PC keyboard will only damage the keyboard itself.

the casing; in a PC, they are often separate. They are connected to sounds circuits on the motherboard.

Is that the lot, then?

That's more or less all you need for a basic computer, yes. Although most computers also contain a **modem** – a set of components (either on the motherboard or connected to it) that allow the computer to send and receive information via digital phone lines and wireless Internet connections. Many also contain extra components such as **sound cards**, **graphics cards** and **video cards**. These are extra chips (or circuit boards) of varying sizes, which plug into the motherboards and provide extra memory and processing power for high-quality sound, graphics, animation, gaming and movie playback. Many computers also have extra **peripheral** (external input or output) **devices** attached, too. These include **printers, scanners, graphics tablets, touchscreens, fingerprint scanners** and more. Many of these devices are linked to the motherboard via **USB ports** – universal 'plugs' that connect peripheral devices to the computer motherboard.

Wow. That's a whole lotta stuff. Maybe 'PC' should stand for 'pretty crowded' or 'positively *crammed*'. 'Personal computer' just doesn't seem to cover it . . .

Activity: Computer Bits and Pieces

Can you match the computer parts on the left to the jobs and functions on the right? I've done the first one for you. See how many you can get. Answers on page 227.

Part	Job
Motherboard	used to input characters and program the computer
RAM	displays text, images and video onscreen
CD drive	the computer's core or central processing unit
Mouse	controls cursor, selects icons and scrolls text
Keyboard	creates a base for most of the computer's essential parts
Monitor	the computer's temporary memory bank
Hard-disk drive	the computer's permanent memory bank
CPU	loads software, saves files, plays music, movies and games

Do computers ever get angry or sad?

*No. Computers can **never** get angry or sad, and never think good or bad things about you. Because, unlike human beings, computers have no **emotions**, and do not really **think** at all. Computer circuits do not reason, judge or understand information the way human brains do. They just calculate and process information using numbers, logic and a complex arrangement of electromagnetic switches.*

Computers don't think?

Nope. Not yet, anyway. One day, we may create truly intelligent 'thinking machines', that reason, learn and interpret the world much as humans do. But for now, at least, even the world's most powerful and 'intelligent' computers are unable to 'think' as we do.

But if they can't *think*, then how can they predict the weather, play cards or beat a human chess champion at their own game?

As complicated as these things seem, none of them really requires thought – only **logic**.

What's that then?

It's a particular method of reasoning. A way of getting definite outputs from definite inputs, simple answers from simple questions, or new information from old (or existing) information.

Hang on – so computers are reasoning, but they're not thinking?

That's right. Because although computers use (or **follow**) logic, the logical reasoning (or thinking behind it) is **not theirs**. It's **given** to them by the human engineers who built the computer chips and circuits in the first place. Here's how it works . . .

Every bit of information a computer handles (or processes) ultimately ends up as a string of **binary code** numbers. Binary code is a way of representing numbers, letters and instructions as a string of 1s and 0s. For example, the letter 'a', translated into binary, is 01100001, while 'b' is 01100010, and 'z' is 01111010. Using this system, you can represent any number, word, phrase or command by sticking these strings of binary code together, like this:

cat	01100011	01100001
	01110100	
3 fat cats	00110011	00100000
	01100110	01100001
	01110100	00100000
	01100011	01100001
	01110100	01110011
the fat cat sat on the mat	01110100	01101000
	01100101	00100000
	01100110	01100001

01110100	00100000
01100011	01100001
01110100	00100000
01110011	01100001
01110100	00100000
01101111	01101110
00100000	01110100
01101000	01100101
00100000	01101101
01100001	01110100

Okay, but what's the point in that? It seems like all you've done is take up more space on the page, and made the words harder to read.

That's true – as a written language, binary code isn't much use. But here's the clever bit: because it only involves two characters (1 and 0), you can use binary code to turn **any** number, word, phrase (even pictures, video clips and pieces of music) into a series of digital, electronic signals.

Think of it like switching a lightbulb on and off, lots and lots of times, very, very quickly. If 'on'=1, and 'off'=0, then you can spell out any word or phrase or command just by flicking the light switch on and off in the right sequence. This, in a way, is what happens inside a computer. Only instead of light switches and light bulbs, computers use electromagnetic switches and tiny pulses of electricity.

Now here's the *really* clever bit: once numbers, words

or other types of information are pulsing through the computer as strings of binary code, they can be split, merged, juggled and compared with each other by running them through **logic gates**. Logic gates are the building blocks of computer circuits. There are many different types, but basically all they do is take one or more binary inputs, compare the input values (1s or 0s) to each other and turn them into a single output (either a 1 or a 0).

You can see a few examples of the most basic logic gates below.

NOT gate (turns an input of 1 into an output of 0, or vice versa)

AND gate (if **both** inputs – A **and** B – are 1s, then the output is 1. Otherwise, the output is 0)

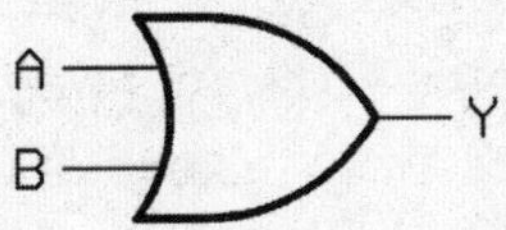

OR gate (if either A **or** B is a 1, then the output is 1. Otherwise, the output is 0)

By linking lots of these gates together, engineers can build complex **logic arrays** inside computers that can process all kinds of complex information. In the early days of computing, these gates took the form of mechanical and electronic relays, which flipped back and forth (like light switches) as they processed pulses of digital information. But ever since the 1970s, logic arrays have been miniaturized and etched into tiny, microscopic circuits inside **microprocessor** chips with no moving parts at all – just tiny, electromagnetic

gates that work by deflecting pulses of electricity using magnetic fields.

With microprocessors, engineers could build more and more complex and intricate arrays, which in turn could process more types of information in more complex ways. This is how today's computers turn a thousand separate temperature and pressure readings into a prediction of tomorrow's weather, or future climate change. It's how a chess computer can take 'inputs' from the arrangement of pieces on a chess board, compare them with arrangements it has 'seen' in other games and turn it all into an 'output' (like a single brilliant chess move) that checkmates a skilled human player. And it's how computers *seem* to be thinking, when all they're *really* doing is **processing**.

So *all* computers today work that way? Even the really big ones?

Pretty much, yes. In the near future, we may build computers that work quite differently. Engineers in Japan and the USA are already working on computers that look and behave more like human brains, with complex artificial neural networks that handle information in more sophisticated ways. Some are even working on biological computers – building computer circuits using growing cells and proteins – in the hope of getting closer to real, thinking, brain-like computers.

Whoa. That sounds a bit freaky. But if computers developed real brains and thinking, couldn't they develop real emotions, too?

It's possible, yes. But don't worry – most experts agree that we're still a *long* way off angry PCs and happy laptops.

That's a relief. It's hard enough getting my computer to boot up as it is. It'd be a real pain if I had to argue with it and keep it happy, too . . .

What language does a computer speak?

Computers do not read, speak or understand languages as we know them. Instead, they read and speak in code, using only the language of logic.

What? That doesn't make much sense.
Why's that?

Well, all computers get *programmed*, right?
Right. Without programming, a computer can't do anything at all. It just sits there, like a very expensive heap of junk.

. . . and that means at *some* point, *someone* has to tell the computer what to do . . .
Yep. That job falls to computer engineers and programmers.

. . . but if computers don't speak our language, then how can anyone tell them what to do?
That's a good point. Let's think about that for a minute. Imagine you had to do a job with someone you'd just met – someone who didn't speak your language at all. Let's say you have to cook a meal, build a gerbil cage or plant a tree in the garden. You need help, but your new friend only speaks Japanese. How would you go about communicating, and getting the job done?

I'd probably show him what I wanted. You know, act it out. Use hand signals and gestures and stuff. Like playing charades.

Good idea. But while that might work well with a person, it wouldn't work at all with a computer. To play charades, or figure out what your play-acted actions might mean, the other player needs to be able to reason, deduce and **think**. And, as we've already learned, computers don't think. Even the world's 'cleverest' computers aren't capable of deciphering sign language. So it'd be impossible to get your instructions across that way.

I suppose I'd have to learn some Japanese, then. Or find someone who could translate.

Right! And that is precisely what engineers and programmers have to do in order to give instructions to computers.

So computers speak Japanese? Wow. I guess that kind of makes sense . . .

Wait – that's not it at all! Computers don't speak Japanese.

Oh. Not even the ones built in Japan?

Errr . . . no. A computer can't 'speak' Japanese any more than it can speak English (or for that matter, French, Spanish or Arabic). As we've already learned, a computer can only really deal with one form of information – binary code. This is the only language (or form of information) a computer can use. Every bit of information inside a computer is converted into strings of 1s and 0s representing numbers, letters and commands, which then flash through computer circuits as a series of electrical pulses.

Wait – does that mean programmers have to learn to speak binary code?

That's what the earliest programmers did, yes. They spent hours flicking switches on and off, or punching holes in pieces of cardboard, to create coded messages and programs that their computers could process. But before too long they realized that this method was too difficult and time-consuming for all but the simplest programming tasks.

Bet it was seriously B-O-R-I-N-G, too.

No doubt. So, to avoid this, they came up with an easier option. Instead of learning computer-ese, they created interpreters and translators that could talk to the computers *for* them. First, they created new **programming languages** based on natural human language and mathematics. This gave programmers a kind of shorthand for common commands like PRINT (which told a computer to display something on the screen), and INPUT or SCAN (which told a computer to wait for input from a keyboard). Then they wrote programs (the hard way, using 1s and 0s) that could translate typed instructions like PRINT into pure binary code, automatically. With this, programmers were freed from all the switching and punching, and could input information directly into the computer as numbers and text.

Over the years, as computer functions (and commands) have become more and more complex, thousands of programming languages have been designed to help translate human instructions into pure binary code. But only a handful of these are used in most modern PCs and laptops. These languages include **BASIC**, **C++**, **COBOL**, **FORTRAN** and **Java**.

Why are there still so many?

Basically, because different people use them for different things.

The most common computer languages fall into one of three groups. **Interpreted languages**, which include **BASIC** and **LISP**, are easy to read and easy to program, but are more limited in what they can do compared with the other groups.

Compiled languages, which include **C++**, **COBOL** and **FORTRAN**, are harder to learn, but much more powerful. Perhaps not surprisingly, most PCs and laptops use compiled languages like this. The third group, **p-code languages**, are somewhere in between the other two. They're pretty fast and powerful, but also fairly easy for human programmers to read, write and understand. This makes them very useful for people who need quick, powerful programs, but don't want to spend years and years learning how to write them. The most common p-code languages are **Java** and **Python**. (Whenever a window on your Internet browser asks you if you want to 'run Javascript', that means there's a program written in Java being run).

That still sounds like quite a hassle. Will we ever be able to just talk to computers, and program them that way?

One day, yes – we probably will. Right now, most speech-recognition programs still have trouble recognizing natural human speech, and are mostly only used for word-processing. Within a few decades, though, computers may start learning *our* languages, rather than the other way around. For more complex programs, engineers will probably still choose to type instructions into computers, just as they do today. For them, it'll be quicker that way. But for the rest of us voice-programming may come in quite handy.

Soon, you'll be telling your computer to add a webpage to your 'favourites' list just by saying 'keep it'. You'll be sending texts and emails just by talking at your laptop. And you'll be training your pet robot by shouting 'sit!', 'stay!' and 'fetch!'.

Now *that's* more like it!

Geekspeak

Computer programmers learn languages like Java to talk to computers. But they also use a whole language of their own when chatting to each other. Abbreviations like LOL, OMG and THX have now made their way into text messages and IMs the world over. But what about these? See how many you can guess correctly. Answers on page 228.

1. **ROFL** means
a) Rolling On the Floor, Laughing
b) Running Out For Lunch
c) Rolling Ostrich Feathers Lightly

2. **NT** means:
a) Nice Tan
b) No Time
c) No, Thanks

3) A **chip head** is:
a) Part of a microprocessor chip
b) Someone who is really into computers
c) Someone who likes fish 'n' chips

4) a **screamer** is:
a) a fast computer
b) a fast programmer
c) a broken loudspeaker

5) a **n00b** is:
a) a type of wireless mouse
b) someone who knows a lot about computers
c) someone new to computing or gaming; a newbie

What is the world's most powerful computer, and what does it do?

Computers are still developing at an incredible pace, so the answer to that question changes every few months. As of 1 January 2011, the world's most powerful was the Chinese supercomputer ***Tianhe-A1****. But other supercomputers in Japan, Europe and the USA weren't far behind.*

It's in China? So what does it do?

Tianhe-A1 lives at the National Supercomputer Centre, in the city of Tianjin, north-east China. There it carries out complicated calculations involved with oil exploration and aircraft simulation. Basically, it takes lots and lots of data from geologists and engineers, and crunches the numbers to help them locate hidden oil reserves deep beneath the sea, and to design bigger, better aeroplanes and rockets. But it could be programmed to do pretty much anything. Tianhe-A1 was first unveiled in 2009, when it immediately took the top spot among the world's most powerful supercomputers. It cost over £50 million to build, fills up an entire room* and takes over 200 people to operate.

---

* Which is kind of funny, when you think about it. I mean, seventy years ago, the first modern computers filled whole rooms. Then we spent decades making them a thousand times smaller, and a billion times more powerful. Yet in 2011, the world's most powerful computer still fills an entire room. That's technology for you.

Whoa. That sounds pretty heavy-duty. So how powerful is it?
Computer processing power is measured in units called **flops**, which is short for **floating point operations per second**. Basically, a flop is a measure of how many calculations a computer can do in a single second. The more flops a computer can do, the more powerful it is considered to be.

I don't get it.
Okay, let's try this . . . QUICKLY – what's 6x6?

Err . . . 36.
Correct. Now if you're like most people, that multiplication probably took you about half a second to answer. If you were a computer, that would give you a processing rate (or **flop count**) of 1 to 2 flops. A basic pocket calculators has a flop count of 10–20. An average PC or laptop processor (or CPU) has a flop count of up to **10 gigaflops** (where 1 gigaflop = **1 billion** flops). This means your home computer can do over 10 billion calculations per second.

Now let's compare this with a supercomputer, and with Tianhe-A1. Most supercomputers have flop counts that are measured in **teraflops**, where one **teraflop** is equal to a **trillion** flops. Tianhe-A1 has a maximum flop rate of **2,570 teraflops** (or **2.57 petaflops**).

That makes Tianhe-A1 roughly **250,000 times**

more powerful than your home computer, and about a **trillion** times faster at sums than you are.

Wow. That's one mean calculator.

Yep. In the number two spot (see the full Top 10 World's Most Powerful Computers list on page 43) for supercomputers is the **Jaguar XT5** (1.75 petaflops) which lives at the Oak Ridge National Laboratory in Tennessee, USA. After that is the **Nebulae Cluster** (1.27 petaflops), found at the National Supercomputing Centre in Shenzen, south-east China. Other 'big boys' include Japan's **Tsubame** (1.19 petaflops), America's **Roadrunner** (1.04 petaflops) and Germany's **Juelich Blue Gene** (825 gigaflops).

What makes these supercomputers so powerful?

In short, lots and lots of super-speedy processor chips, all working together like enormous number-crunching armies. Most home computers contain just one or two core microprocessor chips. Ever since the early development of computers, engineers have been *continually* redesigning and improving them – building smaller, faster and more powerful processors with each passing year. In 1965, computer engineer Gordon Moore predicted that over the next decade the number of components that could be crammed into a single microprocessor chip would **double** every year, bringing with it a doubling in computer processing power and speed. He turned out to be right,* and his predictions about doubling computer power later became known as **Moore's Law**.

In fact, thanks to the rapid development of microchip technology, computer processing power has more or less **doubled every eighteen months** for the last **forty years**. The chances are that engineers have been using Moore's Law as a goal, and that one day the rate of development will start to tail off. But for now, it seems, it shows little sign of slowing down!

Is that what makes them *super*computers, then? They have *super*-powerful processors?

Actually, the processors found in supercomputers are probably little different to the ones in your home PC or laptop. There are just a *lot* more of them. The average PC or laptop contains just 1–4 core processor chips. Those with more than one core chip are called **multi-core processors**, and include **dual-core** (2-chip), **triple-core** (3-chip) and **quad-core** (4-chip) models.

High-performance supercomputers, on the other hand, contain a few more than that. The Tianhe-1A and Jaguar XT5 (currently #1 and #2 on the world's supercomputer list) each contain **over 200,000 processing cores**, spread across thousands

* He also founded the microchip-making company Intel, whose Pentium chips are now found in about eighty per cent of the world's computers, and have made Gordon Moore one of the richest people on the planet. Pretty clever bloke, really.

of interlinked computer **nodes**. Linking up thousands of processors like this allows huge calculations to be split into lots of little ones, which are then carried out simultaneously in different processors, and the results reassembled into a single solution. This is called **parallel computing**, because the calculations are done side by side (or in parallel) in the same computer system. This is what gives supercomputers their serious, digital 'oomph'.

So, if computers are getting twice as powerful every couple of years, how much 'oomph' will they have a hundred years from now?
That's a very good question. With another century of development, computers will likely become **more powerful than we can possibly imagine**.

What will that mean for us? That's another question altogether . . .

Top 10 World's Most Powerful Computers

With computer technology changing so quickly, this list changes almost every month! You can see a full, updated list at http://www.top500.org/

1) **Tianhe 1A** (Tianjin, China) – 2.57 petaflops
2) **Jaguar XT5** (Knoxville, Tennessee, USA) – 1.75 petaflops
3) **Nebulae Cluster** (Shenzen, China) – 1.27 petaflops
4) **Tsubame 2.0** (Tokyo, Japan) – 1.19 petaflops
5) **Hopper XE6** (Berkeley, California, USA) – 1.05 petaflops
6) **Tera-100** (Bruyeres-le-Chatel, France) – 1.05 petaflops
7) **Roadrunner** (Los Alamos, New Mexico, USA) – 1.04 petaflops
8) **Kraken XT5** (Oak Ridge, Tennessee, USA) – 831 gigaflops
9) **Juelich Blue Gene** (Juelich, Germany) – 825 gigaflops
10) **Cielo XE6** (Los Alamos, New Mexico, USA) – 816 gigaflops

What will computers be like in a hundred years' time?

Computers are developing so rapidly that it's difficult – even for experts – to imagine what a twenty-second-century computer will look like. They will certainly be more complex, more powerful and more a part of our everyday lives. They might be built with proteins, with bits of DNA or with tiny packets of light. And the quaint old keyboard-and-mouse one day may be replaced with brain interfaces and thought control . . .

Waaaaaait a minute. Just hold on there, Mr Geekazoid.

What's the matter?

You just said of whole bunch of stuff and, frankly, I have NO idea what it meant. What do you mean they don't know what future computers will look like? Course they do. They're experts, aren't they?

Yes, they are. But they're not psychics.

We've already seen how much computers have changed – going from crude calculators to complex, programmable systems – in the last fifty years alone. And we've seen that, just as Moore's Law predicted, computer processing power is now **doubling** every eighteen months. At that rate of change, it's almost impossible for experts to predict what computers will look like in fifty years' time, let alone a hundred.

Today's supercomputers are about a **billion** times more powerful than those of fifty years ago. So it's fairly safe to say that by the year 2100, computers will be billions (if not **trillions**) of times more powerful than those of today. But for computers to keep developing at that rate we will probably have to change the way we design and build them. So if someone were to bring a twenty-second-century computer back in time* and show it to you today, you probably wouldn't even recognize it as a computer.

Why not?

Well, for starters, they probably won't be built with the same types of electronic chips and circuits you'd find inside a computer today. The speedy development of computers has been based on the ability to make smaller and smaller components and circuits – from the mechanical valves and switches of the early computers to the digital electromagnetic switches on a modern microprocessor chip.

But we're now approaching the limit for how small we can make our microchips. Today's microchips are built (mostly) with layers of silicon, and you can only slice layers of silicon so thinly before they fall apart. So, if engineers are to cram any more components

---

* This is not, by the way, likely to happen. Time-travel – at least into the past – is almost certainly impossible. Otherwise, someone would have already done it. Think about it . . .

on to their chips (and continue to double computer processing power every couple of years), then they'll have to find another way of building them.

Thankfully, computer scientists across the globe are already working on alternative types of processors that could be made far smaller (and therefore far more powerful) than those built with silicon chips.

Like what?

Some are experimenting with building transistors out of tiny tubes less than a thousand times thinner than a human hair, creating the world's first **nanocomputers**. The smallest components found in the microcomputers of today measure about 50 nanometres across. That's **five hundred-thousandths of a millimetre**, or about a **hundred times** thinner than a human hair. Using **nanomaterials** such as **carbon nanotubes**, engineers are already building computer components just 2–3 nanometres wide – more than ten times smaller than those found on today's microchips. These tubular transistors would work in much the same way, just on a much smaller scale.

Others are attempting to make transistors using individual packets of light (or **photons**), creating superfast **photon computers**. Some are even experimenting with bacteria and biological molecules, building organic **biocomputers** by growing bits of protein or DNA on fatty membranes, much like the ones that surround the cells in your body. If that works, then computers might end up looking more like fleshy lungs and livers than boxy, plastic gadgets.

Ewwww, gross! But how could you type on a lung? And where would the mouse plug in?
Well, in future computers, input devices like the keyboard, mouse and touch-screen may well be replaced with voice recognition modules, or even mind-reading brain-computer interfaces (or BCIs) that allow you to type and browse the Internet with your thoughts alone.

You mean control a computer just with your brain? Like telepathy?
Something like that, yes.

Is that even possible?
Not only is it possible, it has already been done. For some time now, neuroscientists have been experimenting with using brainwave sensors to control computers and other electronic devices. EEGs (or Electro-encephalograms) have been used by scientists and doctors for decades, in order to monitor electrical patterns (i.e brainwaves) in patients and test subjects. You've probably seen them on TV. Basically, sensor wires (or a cap covered with sensor wires) is placed on the patient's head, which measure electricity conducted through the skull and display the brainwaves on a computer monitor.

Well, by attaching those sensors to different types of devices, you can do more than just display your brainwaves – you can use them to control things. A few years back, we had the first thought-controlled computer cursor, or 'telepathic mouse', which allowed people with full-body paralysis to move an onscreen cursor up, down, left and right. Now, computer software company G-Tec have released the first thought-controlled **typing** interface, called **Intendix**.

This works by displaying a screenful of keyboard characters (letters, numbers, space bar and so on), and lighting each one up, in turn, with a series of quick flashes. The user wears a brainwave-measuring EEG cap, and stares at the letter they want. When they see their chosen letter light up, it causes a brief 'jump' in their brainwaves. This is picked up by the EEG, relayed to a word processing or email program and used to type that letter in a document or message.

That's just crazy.

It's crazy, but it works. With practice, users can type at a rate of one letter per second. This is still very slow compared with regular keyboard typing or speech. And for now, it's only really useful for disabled people who cannot move, speak or communicate in other ways. But, in time, this technology will likely develop to the point where you can 'type' whole words, sentences and messages in seconds, with your thought alone. Soon, you'll be pinging friends and updating your webpage just by thinking about it. . .

That sounds almost like magic!

Well, as the great science-fiction writer Arthur C. Clarke once said, 'Any sufficiently advanced technology is indistinguishable from magic.' With enough time to develop, computer technology could make 'magical' things like mind control and thought-messaging a part of our everyday future lives.

It also sounds a bit scary. I mean, you'd have to be very careful. You wouldn't want everything you thought about turning up online, would you?

Nahhh, I'm sure it'd be fine . . .

[Oh, look, there's Dave! Hey, Dave!]

[Howzitgoin'?]

[Not bad. I haven't changed my underpants in three days.]

[Wait – what?]

[Oops.]

[LOL]

2.
Signals, Codes and Smartphones

How did people talk before telephones?

Before modern telephones, staying in touch long-distance was very tricky. There were many ways to do it, including runners, riders, flags and fires. But these ancient messaging systems were all pretty slow and unreliable. It wasn't until the discovery of electricity – and the invention of the telegraph – that truly 'instant' messages became possible.

Wow. That all sounds pretty complicated.
Well, staying in touch at a distance is a pretty complicated business. In today's twenty-first-century world, making calls, or sending texts, emails and IMs – is simple. We take it all for granted. But think about it – how would you contact your mates in a world without mobile phones and computer networks?

Easy. Most of my mates live on the same street. I could just yell really loudly out of my window.
Perhaps. But I doubt you yelling IM-style updates* out of the window every half-hour would go down too well

* To test this theory, I just yelled this out of my back window: 'WRITING A NEW BOOK ABOUT COMPUTERS AND STUFF!! *FRINGE* ON TV TONIGHT! SWEET!' My next-door neighbour does not look pleased.

with your parents. Or your neighbours. And what if you had a message for someone further away? Like a few streets over, or on the other side of town?

Well, I'd just leg it over there.

Right – good idea. And in fact, for most of history, that's pretty much what people did. They would either leg it over to someone's home to deliver the message in person, or give the message to a foot messenger, or 'runner', to pass on for them. In ancient Greece, the hardiest long-distance 'runners' would run up to 30 miles in a single day to deliver important messages – like war reports from commanders on distant front lines. This later gave rise to the long-distance 'marathon' races of the Greek Olympic games. And in medieval Japan war reports and secret messages were carried by ninjas!

No way!

It's true. While some ninjas dabbled in assassination and undercover spy work, most were just foot messengers with legendary speed and endurance (in Japanese, the word *nin-ja* actually means 'endurance man'). So in a way they were the world's deadliest postmen!

Cool. Wish I had a ninja postman. Mine is totally boring.
Me, too.

But what if you had to get a message to someone, like, right away? Like in an emergency or something? Or right in the middle of a battle?
In ancient battles, many generals and commanders would send orders between troops or ships via flags with special colours and patterns. Others used loud blasts of sound – trumpeting signals through horns or shells.

But of course there's only so far you can see a flag or hear a horn blast. And even the speediest ninjas and messengers took hours or days to deliver messages cross-country (and if you were 'calling' internationally, then we're talking months or years). You could speed a message up a bit by sending it on horseback (like the famous 'Pony Express' of the wild American west), or attaching it to the leg of a trained hawk or carrier pigeon. But it was practically impossible to send an instant message over a very long distance.

But what if you really had to contact someone right away, and they were, like, over a hundred miles away?

Well, for the most part you just couldn't. And that's how it stayed for a long, long time.

Why's that?

Well, for starters, there wasn't much need for the high-speed, long-distance messaging systems we have today. News just arrived whenever it arrived, and there really weren't too many reasons for trying to make it arrive any faster. Except – once again – battle reports in warfare.

Some cunning systems were invented for this purpose. Native American tribes, for example, used fires or smoke signals to send messages between villages and mountaintops. And similar chains of 'fire signals' were used to signal between the English coastal forts (or Martello towers) during the Napoleonic wars, and between distant forts along the Great Wall of China.

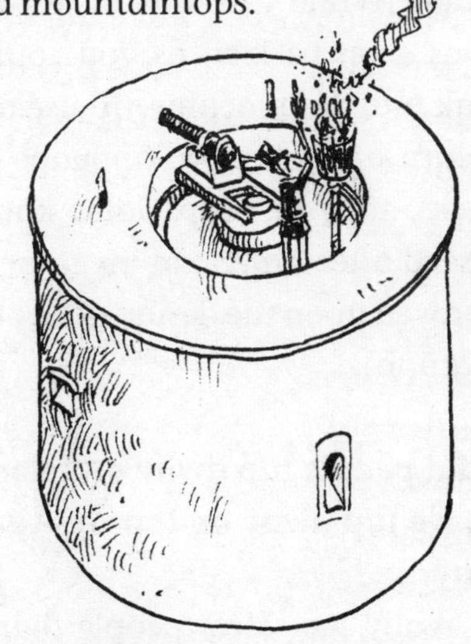

But, for the most part, people just accepted that it took days, months or years to get messages about. And it pretty much stayed that way right up until the ninteenth century.

Why's that? What happened then?

It was round about then that people began figuring out how electricity and magnetism worked. Along the way, a few particularly clever folks discovered that you could use electricity to transmit and receive messages – almost instantaneously – over very long distances.

In 1837, the electric telegraph was invented by British engineers William Cooke and Charles Wheatstone. This used a system of magnetic coils to send messages through wires in the form of an electric current. While this was faster than sending letters, it was a bit trickier, as you couldn't simply type or speak into the machine. To use a telegraph, you had to learn a whole new language – a system of coded knocks, taps or beeps later known as Morse Code (named after American inventor Samuel Morse, who improved upon the design of Cooke and Wheatstone's telegraph).

So did people tap away on telegraphs at home, like we tap away on laptops to send emails today?

Not really, no. Most people didn't have access to a

telegraph in their own homes. Even if they did, few could be bothered with learning the coding systems used to send and receive messages. Instead, trained telegraph operators had to tap messages out at one end of the wire and decode them into written words at the other. So you had to pay an operator to send the message for you, at a public telegraph station, usually at the post office. It was electric mail, but it certainly wasn't email . . .

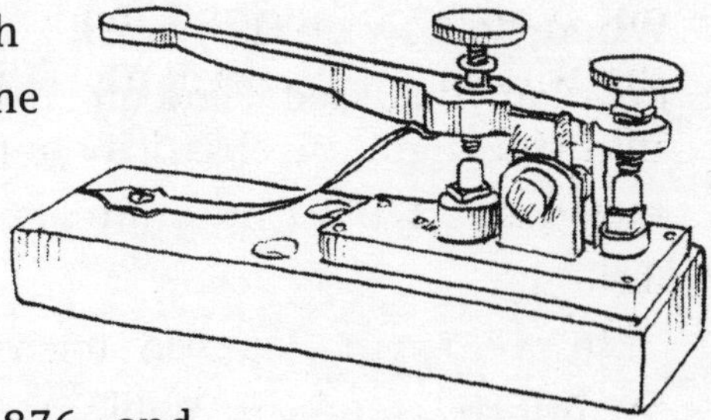

It wasn't until 1876, and the invention of the electric telephone, that long-distance messaging got a bit more user-friendly. Three engineers – Antonio Meucci, Elisha Gray and Alexander Graham Bell – all invented types of electric telephone. All three were based upon the idea of using a magnet to convert the human voice into a series of electric signals, which could then be sent through wires just like telegraphs. But it was Bell's telephone design that eventually caught on.

By the late 1800s, there were hundreds of thousands of Bell's electric telephones connecting businesses and households throughout Europe and America. The age of the modern phone call had arrived. Then in 1895 Italian engineer Guglielmo Marconi built the first wireless (or radio) transmitter and receiver. Marconi's wireless telegraphs were initially used to communicate with ships out at sea, but they later evolved into two-way 'talk radios' used by military commanders, and eventually into the wireless telephone and communications networks we all enjoy today.

Whoa. So how do they work?

I'm glad you asked. Read on . . . .

Do It Yourself: build your own electric telegraph!

Make your own telegraph for sending secret messages between rooms. You might need help to find the bits and pieces you need at the shops. But, once you're all hooked up, you'll have your very own secret telegraph system.

What you'll need

- 2 bits of cardboard, about 20 cm x 10 cm
- 2 more bits of cardboard, about 3 cm x 8 cm
- 3 lengths of wire, about 20 cm long
- 3 longer pieces of wire (long enough to trail between two rooms)
- 1 battery (D size)
- 4 drawing pins
- 2 electric buzzers (you can buy these in electrical shops)
- pencil, scissors, pliers and sticky tape

How to do it

To make the first transmitter (or 'sounder'):

1. Take one large piece of cardboard, draw a line down the centre, dividing it in half, width-ways. This will be your sounder base.
2. Take one small piece of cardboard, put a bend in it about 2 cm from one end, then tape that end to the base, close to (and parallel to) one short edge of the base. This will be your signalling switch. To complete it, push one drawing pin into the base (just beneath the free, flapping end of the switch) and the other into the underside of the flapping end above. When you press the switch down, the heads of the two drawing pins should now click together.
3. Find a spot on the opposite side of the base, and tape the buzzer there.
4. Place the battery on the line you drew in step 1, and tape it down to the base (leaving the ends free).
5. Now take one short wire, tape one end to the base (i.e. the flat end) of the battery, and connect the other end to the buzzer – twist it around one of the wires sticking out of the buzzer, and tape them together.
6. Now take the other short wire, tape one end to the battery base (make sure it's touching metal, and not just tape), wrap the other end tightly

around the drawing pin. Lift up the base, look underneath, and use the pliers to bend the tip of the pin over, so it won't slip out (get a parent to help with this).

To make the second transmitter:
Take the other large piece of cardboard, and repeat steps 1–3 above.

1. Take another short wire, wrap one end around the lower drawing pin (as before) and connect the other to the buzzer (wrapping and taping it, as before).
2. Place it in another room to transmitter #1.

Now connect the two transmitters together:
Take three of your long wires and run them between the two rooms, placing the ends close to the two transmitters. Use the first long wire to connect the **buzzer of transmitter #2** to the **upper pin** of the switch on **transmitter #1** (again, bend the end of the pin over with pliers to stop it falling out).

Use the second wire to connect the **buzzer of transmitter #1** to the **upper pin** of the switch **on transmitter #2.**

Finally, use the third wire to connect the **free (positive) end of the battery** on transmitter #1 to the **lower pin on transmitter #2.**

That's it! You're done. Now you can tap out secret messages in Morse Code between the two rooms,

plan secret meetings or launch your plot to take over the world. Whatever you fancy. See below for a complete Morse Code letter map to use.

Morse Code letter map

A	.–	P	.––.
B	–...	Q	––.–
C	–.–.	R	.–.
D	–..	S	...
E	.	T	–
F	..–.	U	..–
G	––.	V	...–
H	....	W	.––
I	..	X	–..–
J	.–––	Y	–.––
K	–.–	Z	––..
L	.–..	Period	.–.–.–
M	––	Comma	––..––
N	–.	Out	.–.–. (message ends)
O	–––		

How do sounds squeeze through phone lines?
They don't. Sounds are waves of vibrating air, which can't really travel through miles of metal or plastic telephone cable. Instead, modern telephones translate sounds into coded signals, which are then transmitted through phone lines as pulses of electricity or light.

What do you mean, 'sounds can't travel through telephone cables'? Course they can. How else could we hear our phone calls?
It's true, they can't. And here's the simple test to prove it. Imagine that you unplugged the cable from your home telephone, and got a friend across town to do the same . . .

Hang on a minute – how can you call him and tell him what to do when you've just unplugged the phone?
What? I don't know . . . you'd have to use mobile text messages or IMs or something. To be honest, it doesn't really matter, since I don't want you to actually do the experiment, anyway. You can just imagine it, and the result will be obvious.

Oh, okay. In that case, you may continue.
Why, thank you. Very gracious. Now, where was I? Ah, yes . . .

. . . Now hold the end of the unplugged cable a few centimetres in front of your face, and get your friend to hold his end of the cable close to his ear. Then you SHOUT AS LOUD AS YOU CAN into the end of the cable: 'HELLO? HELLO? MR WATSON – COME HERE, I NEED YOU.'* If your friend hears it, he has to come over.

. . . Or send you a text on his mobile?

Right. Whatever. The point is, do you think it would work?

Ha! Don't be stupid! Of course not!

But why not? I mean, there must be a phone line connecting your house to your friend's house, right? And you've just made a sound at one end of it. So why didn't the sound travel through and reach your friend's ear at the other end?

Duhhh!! Because the phones were unplugged!! And you need the phones to pick up the sound and . . . err . . . well, you know . . . .they . . . errr . . . Hmmmm. Good point. What exactly do telephones do?

Telephones receive sounds (or waves of air pressure) and translate them into electrical signals. Signals which can be transmitted over long distances, with the use of electricity and electromagnetic radiation.

---

* This, apparently, was the first thing ever spoken into a working telephone – by telephone inventor Alexander Graham Bell, to his lab assistant, Thomas A. Watson. So there you go.

I don't get it.

Okay, think of it this way. Sounds are just wobbles or waves of pressure in the air. Whenever you pluck a guitar string or blow air into the mouthpiece of a saxophone, you're making something vibrate (i.e. the string or the reed inside the mouthpiece), which in turn vibrates the air around it. This goes for speech sounds, too. When you speak, shout or sing, you're blowing air past the taut, stringy **vocal cords** in your throat, which vibrate the air inside your mouth and nose, and send wobbly air waves out in all directions.

Some of these wobbling airwaves may then reach the ear of a listener. Here, the airy vibration is carried into the ear canal, where it wobbles the eardrum, the bones behind the eardrum, and finally thousands of tiny, pressure-sensitive hairs deep in the inner ear. These hairs trigger a pattern of signals, which your brain then translates into 'guitar', 'saxophone' or 'MR WATSON – COME HERE, I NEED YOU'. Got it?

Got it.

Good. Okay – now here's the tricky bit. Ordinarily, these soundwaves can't travel very far through the air. So if you're hoping to chat quietly at a distance of over six metres, then you're pretty much stuffed. They do, however, travel a bit better through (thicker, denser) liquids and solids.* So one way of making a long-distance sound device (or a basic telephone) is to thread a piece of string between two soup tins (or plastic cups), pull the string taut and then talk into one end to make the solid string vibrate (see below). Here, the solid string vibrates, and passes the soundwaves to the air in the listener's cup (and ear). And it works over a much greater distance than you'd think.

* This is why doctors use solid, metal stethoscopes to listen for your heartbeat, and why nosy people press their ears to wine glasses held against walls, to listen in on their neighbours.

Do It Yourself: make your own (rubbish) telephone

- Get a piece of string and two empty soup cans or plastic cups (cans work better).
- Punch a hole at the bottom of each can (get a parent to help with this). Make the holes just large enough to put the string through – no larger.
- Pass the string through the hole of one can or cup, tie a fat knot in it, then pull the string tight so that the knot rests in the bottom of the can.
- Thread the other end of the string through the bottom of the other can, make a knot and pull.
- Place the open end of one can over your ear and have your partner speak into the open end of the other can.
- Bingo – one rubbish telephone. It's made of rubbish, and it sounds rubbish. Genius, eh?

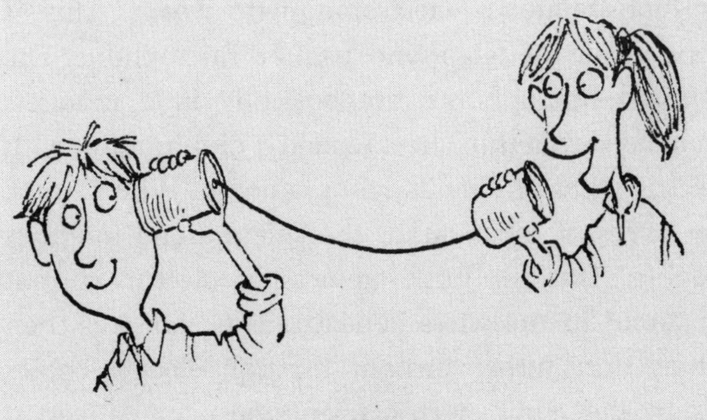

Cool. But that's not how proper telephones work, right?

Right. Over longer distances (like across town), it would be very difficult to keep the string tight enough to carry the vibration well. Even if you could, by the time you'd strung a thin, high-tension line from every phone in town to every other you'd end up with a tangled web of dangerous, bird-bothering tripwires. Moreover, every time one wire crossed or touched another, the vibrations would interfere with each other, garbling the sounds beyond all recognition. All in all, hardly worth the hassle.

No, to cover longer distances – and complicated networks – strings carrying wobbling soundwaves just aren't going to cut it. Instead, you have to convert your soundwaves into something else. And that's where electric (and now digital electronic) telephones come in. Modern phones translate (or convert) airy, vibrating soundwaves into pulses of electricity, light or high-frequency electromagnetic waves. This is done inside the telephone, using a microphone. The simplest microphones are basically little magnets embedded in a thin sheet (called a diaphragm), with electric wires or circuits lying beneath. When struck by waves of airy sound, the microphone magnets wobble. This, in turn, creates an electric current or signal in the wires beneath. This signal is then either transmitted straight through electric cables (as in the early electric telephones), or converted into pulses of light, radio waves or microwaves before being beamed via fibre-optic cables, satellites and antennas to a receiving telephone many miles away.

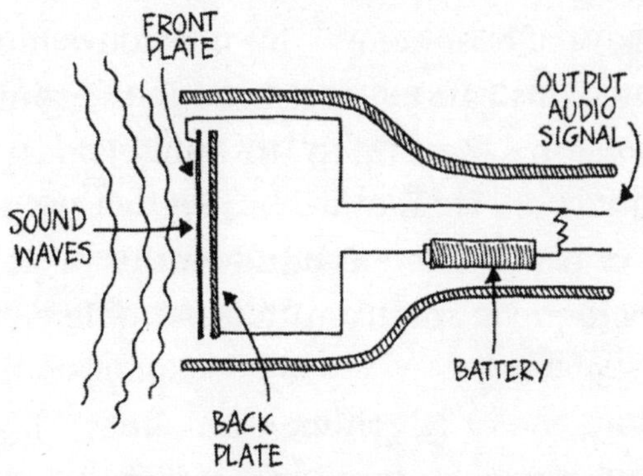

But how does that help? I mean, we can't hear electricity or light when it comes out the other end, can we?

Right. If this was the end of the story, then all we'd have to show for our troubles would be a dull buzzing sound and a dimly illuminated earhole. But here, fortunately, is where electric or electronic loudspeakers come in. Speakers are a bit like microphones in reverse. When the telephone signal arrives at the speaker, waves of electricity pulse through wires beneath a speaker magnet, causing the magnet to wobble and create waves of pressure (i.e. soundwaves) in the air around it. These soundwaves then happily enter your ears and wobble your eardrums – as if the sound was coming from a metre away, rather than across several miles, countries or continents.

But don't the waves and things still get all mixed up and garbled when the phone lines connect together?
Incredibly, no – they don't. This was a problem in the early days of telephones.* But nowadays hundreds of separate calls can be sent through the same cables, by staggering the timing (in milliseconds) of when the signals are sent, attaching special codes to each signal or using different **bandwidths** (or parts of the electromagnetic spectrum) to send different types of signal.

In fact, major telephone trunk lines – like the 23-mile undersea cable that connects the UK to mainland Europe – now carry thousands of separate, coded telephone conversations at once, along with pictures, video and trillions of bytes of website and computer data. Just try doing all that with plastic cups and bits of string. Not easy.

Yeah. Plus you'd get nosy fish listening in on your phone calls.
Err . . . right. We couldn't have that, could we?

---

* One that people used to call 'crossed wires'. Which is why we still use that phrase to describe mixed-up or miscommunicated information today.

How do mobile phones find each other?

They send out signals to tell their local mobile phone networks (or grids) where to find them. To connect a phone call between them, a computer-controlled exchange system lends them a pair of radio channels to chat, and bounces radio waves, microwaves and digital electronic signals back and forth as you talk.

All that happens every time you call someone?
Yep. Every time.

Wow. That seems like an awful lot of bother just for a quick phone call.
I suppose it is. But I guess most people (well, most mobile-phone fans, anyway) would say it was worth it. Besides it all happens so fast you don't even notice. You just dial (or select) a number, and within a two or three seconds the call is connected automatically. One second later, a suitably irritating ringtone starts blaring out on your friend's phone. Provided that they pick it up, you're now ready to blather away about nothing and everything – blissfully unaware of all the switching, bouncing and beaming of electromagnetic signals that are making your conversation possible.

But why do we have to bother with all that switching and beaming and stuff?
How d'you mean?

I mean, two old-school telephones were connected by a single cable, right? So why can't we just replace that one cable with one wireless signal, and be done with it?
That's a very good question. In fact, the simplest (and earliest) wireless telephones did just that. In a way, the first 'mobile phones' were two-way radios used to communicate between ports and ships. But (once again) it was war that really drove the development of this new technology, and by World War Two portable two-way radios (or 'walkie-talkies') became small enough to be carried by soldiers on the battlefield.

Like modern mobiles, each walkie-talkie handset contained a **microphone**, a **speaker**, a **battery**, an **antenna**, and an electronic **radio transmitter and receiver**. To 'call' a pal with a walkie-talkie, you had to agree (before you set off) on the exact radio channel (or frequency) you would be using. Then

you simply tuned the radio to that channel to receive signals, and pushed a button to transmit (or talk back) on the same channel. For most purposes, this worked just fine. In fact, thousands of soldiers, lorry drivers, police officers, paramedics and fire-fighters are still using these two-way radio systems today.

So what was the problem with those? Why don't we all just use walkie-talkies, then, just like soldiers and policemen? That would be seriously *cool*!

Well, walkie-talkies work fine if only one person needs to talk at a time. But since both 'callers' in a two-way radio exchange are using the same radio channel for both **talking** and **listening**, you can't do both these things at once. If you try to 'butt in' and talk while someone else is still transmitting, your message will either be lost altogether or (at the very least) garbled or cut off, mid-sentence. To get around this, two-way radio users have to take turns talking and use special codes to tell the listener when they've finished a message or conversation. That's why most walkie-talkie conversations sound like this:

Shhhhhhhhhh (click) 'Victor Alpha Tango, this is Golf Juliet Mike . . . OVER.'

Shhhhhhhhhh (click) 'Golf Juliet Mike, this is Victor Alpha Tango . . . hello, Glenn . . . OVER.'

Shhhhhhhhhh (click) 'Hello, Vicky . . . listen – can you pick up a pizza on the way home? . . . OVER.'

Shhhhhhhhhh (click) 'Is that it? Just a pizza?. . . OVER.'

Shhhhhhhhhh (click) 'Errr, no actually . . . I've been thinking, and I don't want you to be my girlfriend any more . . . It's just too difficult going out with a policewoman . . . It's over!'

Shhhhhhhhhh (click) 'I'm sorry . . . it's – what? OVER.'

Shhhhhhhhhh (click) 'I said "it's over" . . . OVER.'

Shhhhhhhhhh (click) 'What do you mean, "it's over-over"? You're not making any sense . . . OVER.'

Shhhhhhhhhh (click) 'No, no, no . . . not "over-over". Just "over" . . . As in "we're finished" . . . or "I want to break up with you" . . . OVER.'

Shhhhhhhhh (click) 'Oh . . . well in that case, you can get your own pizza. OVER AND OUT.'

Well . . . something like that, anyway.

Very funny. So how are mobile phones any different?

Modern mobile phones get around this by using a *pair* of radio channels (or frequencies) to communicate back and forth. When a call is placed, and two mobile phones are connected, they are automatically assigned (or tuned to) a pair of radio frequencies – one to send, one to receive. So each phone can transmit and receive simultaneously, and the speakers are free to butt in whenever they like, without fear of cutting each other off. (And they can forget about all that irritating 'OVER' stuff).

Okay, but that still doesn't explain why you need all that computerized switching and bouncing you talked about at the beginning. What's all that for?

That's all done for two reasons.

The **first** is to prevent **interference** from other callers.

If you think about it, in a big city like London, Tokyo or New York, at any given time a million or more people may be trying to make mobile phone calls *all at once*. Even in smaller towns, the number of

simultaneous callers could number in the thousands. So, if all these people tried to connect through the same two 'transmit' and 'receive' radio channels, they'd end up in one seriously confusing conversation! With so many people making calls at once, it'd be pretty much impossible to find a 'free' channel (or frequency) by yourself, no matter how many times you tried switching (or tuning) to a new one. And no reasonable number of human telephone operators could connect a million calls all being made at the same time.

So, to get around this, mobile calls are relayed through local networks to powerful computers at **central** (or **main**) **exchanges**. There, free channels (or pairs of radio frequencies) are automatically found and assigned to each call being placed, usually within one or two seconds!

Okay. So what's the other reason?

The **second** reason for all the switching and relaying is to keep the call signal **clear and strong**, even when the two mobile phones are widely separated from each other. With two-way radios (or walkie-talkies) you have to rely on the strength of the transmitters and receivers to send signals back and forth. In individual handsets, these aren't very powerful, which is why simple, two-way walkie-talkies can only be used over fairly short distances.

You can, of course, increase this distance by using

a powerful, central transmitter and receiver. Most police stations and army bases house powerful radio transmitters and receiving antennas for this very reason. Even so, the further you get from the central transmitter/receiver, the weaker the signal becomes. So if you want to get a clear signal to a phone out in the countryside – or connect two phones in two distant cities – you're going to need a better system.

Like what?

Well, that's where mobile phone **networks** come in. In each mobile phone network, there's usually a single, **main exchange** in every major city – just like the police station or army HQ described above. But to get a clear signal to areas outside the city the main exchange is connected to a number of local exchanges, which boost call transmissions and relay them on to local antennas (or 'cell towers'). These towers are dotted all over the landscape, and together divide it up into a grid of invisible, overlapping circles (or cells). Each cell* has a cell tower in the centre, whose range crosses over with that of its neighbouring towers. If you could see this grid of overlapping radio transmitter ranges, it would look a bit like a honeycomb in a beehive.

---

* *This*, of course, is why mobile phones are also known as 'cellphones'. Not because you're allowed to use them in prison or something.

So when you place a call it's not quite as simple as sending a radio wave from one phone to another. Rather, each phone sends a radio signal to its nearest cell tower (this happens continuously while your phone is switched on, whether you're making a call or not). From there, the radio signals are transferred (usually as an electric signal, through an underground cable) to their local exchanges, which in turn relay the signal onward (via cables or microwave transmitters) to a central main exchange, often in a neighbouring city. In this way, the main exchange can keep track of where everybody's phone is, all the time.*

When a call is placed, a signal is relayed from one phone to the main exchange, which locates the other phone (which, as we've just learned, is constantly 'pinging' the main exchange from local cells), assigns a pair of frequencies for them to communicate over and connects them up in the middle. From that point on, signals are relayed between cells, towers and exchanges as radio waves, microwaves and pulses of electricity.

Microwaves? Yikes! Is that why some people think that mobile phones melt your brain?
Part of it, yes.

---

* In fact, police detectives, spies and nosy parents with the right equipment can 'trace' your location this way – and find out where you are just by following your mobile phone signal!

Do they?

Not as far as we know, no.

For one thing, mobile phones don't actually emit microwaves. While mobile phone exchanges (i.e. local and central exchange towers) do communicate this way, mobiles use **low frequency radio waves**. Radio waves are a form of **non-ionizing radiation**, which means that (unlike X-rays and ultraviolet rays), they can't break through the skin, penetrate your cells and damage the DNA inside. And while mobile phones fall somewhere between TVs and microwaves in the *type* of radiation they chuck out, they operate at **tiny power levels** (around 1 watt – or about a hundredth the power of a bright home light bulb) and emit only **tiny amounts** of radiation.

Also – if you think about it – **hundreds of millions** of people have been using mobile phones for **decades**, now. Yet most scientific studies have revealed **no effect** at all on the brains of mobile phone users. So, while we can't know for certain that cellphones do no damage at all, we can be fairly sure that they don't actually *melt your brain*.

Drat. Guess I'll have to find another excuse for not doing my maths homework, then. Come to think of it – does *maths* melt your brain? It certainly feels like it . . .

Police Codes Puzzle

When police officers call in number plates and soldiers radio map positions to each other, they use special words to represent the letters of the alphabet, so that they're not misheard or misunderstood. This is called the Phonetic Alphabet. 'AB1 GHC', for example, would be said 'Alpha Bravo one, Golf Hotel Charlie'. Learn the system for yourself by solving all the clues in this word-search puzzle. Answers on page 228.

Alpha	Bravo	Charlie
Delta	Echo	Foxtrot
Golf	Hotel	India
Juliet	Kilo	Lima
Mike	November	Oscar
Papa	Quebec	Romeo
Sierra	Tango	Uniform
Victor	Whisky	X-ray
Yankee	Zulu	

T U K M U U O F V M R R C H A R L I E T
K U A X Z U L U D I T S E E G A L Q N O
E M B Z D N O X V Z M G B I I G T N O J
A P A P S I E R R A K M E X M E H L V S
L L R M K F X W O O D N U D R O G I E F
P E N G A O H R E C H O Q O T D Y R M D
H A Z K E R L M O G N A T E S T N Y B K
A V J R B M O A B A H C L O E C M L E X
S U E M V R I J D D I J I V R Z A P R V
R M X Z K K A K N V N W M L Q T L R V G
A G F R G U I V E Y D F A A E T X R A Y
J Z F O X Z J L O O I Q N A T Y U O T P
J U L I E T Z Y O W A Y V P A H W R F Q
K F W H I S K Y Y A N K E E E Q I G Q Z

Can aliens hear our phone calls in Space?

It's possible, yes. After all, communication signals from Earth have already travelled trillions of miles into Space, in all directions. So if someone – or something – were out there listening they could well pick our signals up. But whether they'd be able to recognize them as 'phone calls', or do anything about it, is quite another story.

Wow. Our signals can really travel that far?

Absolutely. The *Voyager 1* space probe, launched in 1977, has now travelled almost 11 billion miles from Earth. We're still sending commands to it via radio signals. Travelling at the speed of light (as all electromagnetic radiation does), these signals take over sixteen hours to arrive. But arrive they do.

While the *Voyager* signals are beamed out into Space on purpose, plenty more get beamed out there by accident. The Earth's atmosphere traps or absorbs certain types of radiation – including gamma rays, X-rays and ultraviolet rays.* But other types – including certain ranges (or frequencies) of microwaves and radio waves – can pass through, and travel through the atmosphere in both directions. That means we are constantly receiving radio and

---

* And a good thing, too. If it didn't, X-rays and gamma rays from the Sun and other nearby stars would bathe the planet in deadly levels of radiation, and life could not survive.

microwave signals from way out in Space, while radio waves and microwaves that originate from Earth are beamed out into the Universe in all directions.

Calls between land-lines, and a good number of our cellphone calls, travel mostly through Earth-bound cables or low-powered microwave towers,* and it's unlikely that many of *these* signals are strong enough to make it out of the atmosphere. Other signals get beamed towards communications satellites in orbital Space, which receive the signals and bounce

---

* For more about how cell phones work, see 'How do mobile phones find each other?' on page 69.

them back to Earth. But these radio and microwaves can't be focused into narrow enough beams to hit the satellites precisely. Instead, a good part of each wave washes past the satellites and out into Space. If they're listening, *these* are the phone calls that the aliens will pick up. Along with an assortment of broadcasts from Earthbound TV and radio stations, global-positioning-system signals and computer data.

Hang on a minute – if our phone signals are beaming out all over the place, and bouncing off the atmosphere and stuff, then how come we can't hear them all buzzing away in the air all around us?

That's because without special equipment human beings can only hear a very narrow range of electromagnetic (or EM) waves. Our ears can only detect EM waves with wavelengths of between 1.7 cm and 17 metres, which we hear as high and low-pitched sounds. Some animals can hear sounds we can't, because they can detect wavelengths outside of these ranges. Elephants and whales, for example, can hear lower sounds with longer wavelengths, known as **infrasound**. Others, including bats, moths and some birds, can hear higher sounds with shorter wavelengths, known as **ultrasound**.

But no animal on the planet can hear phone calls transmitted as radio waves or microwaves with

their ears alone. It takes a device (like a radio set, or mobile phone) with a receiver and loudspeaker to pick up these signals and translate them into sound waves before we can actually hear them. Otherwise, the radio and microwave signals lie outside of the range our ears can recognize. Which is why a) we need phones to hear phone calls, and b) we aren't driven insane by a million telephone conversations reaching our ears all day long.

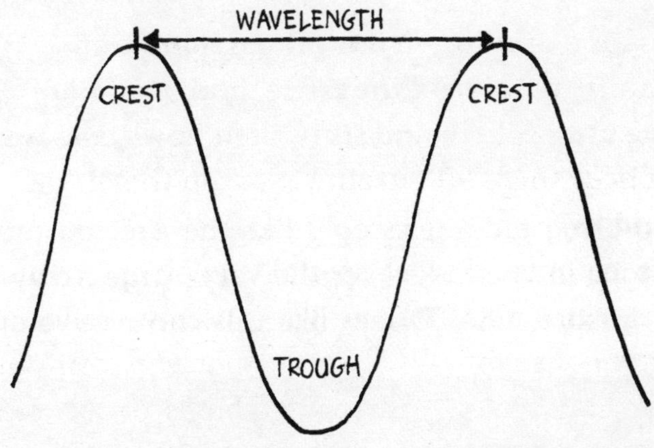

Okay, so could aliens hear radio waves and microwaves with their alien ears? Is that how they could hear those signals beamed out into Space?

It's possible, I suppose. But, more likely, they would listen for them the same way astronomers on Earth do – using massive receiving dishes and signal converters. Scientists and engineers working on the Search for Extraterrestrial Intelligence (SETI) project

do so using radio telescopes like the **Arecibo** radio telescope in Puerto Rico, or the **Very Large Array** in New Mexico, USA. Dishes like this can receive and

translate radio and microwave signals from trillions of miles away. If alien astronomers are listening out for signs of *us*, then they're probably doing it using a similar type of device.

Yikes! But what if they *do* hear us, and they decide to invade us or something?

That's possible, but it doesn't seem very likely. Even if our signals did make it across trillions of miles of Space to arrive at alien listening devices, there's a good chance that they wouldn't understand what they were hearing.

Why? Because they wouldn't speak our language?

More than that – they might not even recognize that it *was* a language, or even a sign of life. On the way out of the Earth's atmosphere, any signal leaving the planet would be **distorted** (think 'fuzzy TV or radio broadcast') by the atmosphere itself. Then, on its journey of millions of miles through Space, the signal would weaken (or **attenuate**) as it passed through thin, interstellar gas-clouds and was partly absorbed by the gas molecules within. Once the signal finally arrived at the alien 'Arecibo', it would do so alongside radio signals from thousands of stars, galaxies, black holes and other celestial objects, creating **interference**, and making it hard to pick out our signal from all the others.

Now let's say that the signal has survived all that, some alien astronomer has recognized it as an alien (or rather, some *extra-planetary* astronomer – since we would be the aliens!) phone call, and set about organizing an invasion party. Even if they had spacecraft that could travel at close to the speed of light, it would most likely take millions of years to cover the millions of light years between them and us. A lot can happen in a million years. In that time, humankind might have already left the planet, or destroyed ourselves completely. And if we were still here, then we'd have had a million years or so to develop better technology, so we'd probably be in good shape to defend ourselves from alien invaders, anyway.

But what if they flew through some wormhole in Space, and arrived here next week or something? What then?!

Then we might be in trouble. Better be careful what you say about aliens on the phone, just in case . . .

What makes smartphones so smart?

In short: microchips, operating systems and downloadable programs. Modern smartphones are more like miniature mobile computers than telephones. A mobile phone is just a handy communication device. But a smartphone is a super-versatile digital toolbox, which can be used for everything from homework and hobbies to push-ups and zit-popping.

A smartphone could do my homework? All right!

Well . . . no phone is smart enough (at least not yet) to *do* your homework *for* you. But they can help you get it done. Need to Google the population of Turkmenistan while you're sitting on the bus? Done. Need help plotting a graph for maths class? No problem. Need to translate something from English into Spanish? Too easy. Forgotten which bit of homework was due in first? There's an 'app' for that, too.

But how can they do all that stuff? I mean, a smartphone is basically just a fancy mobile phone, right?

The early ones were, perhaps. But today's smartphones are far more than that. For all their fancy names and trendy designs, mobile phones are still just two-way, wireless communication devices. They're designed to connect two people across a wireless cellphone network, via simple talk or text message. More sophisticated mobiles may also have cameras, mp3 players and some limited ability to surf the Web. But that's about it.

Smartphones, on the other hand, are the digital equivalent of a Swiss Army knife – they come in handy for *all sorts* of things. With a smartphone, you can make video calls, browse *any* website, update your blog or Twitter feed, play games online, get directions using the global positioning system (GPS), watch movies, buy music, even scan your fingerprints. What's more, smartphones are user-programmable. New uses and applications (or **apps**) are being written by software programmers all the time, which can be downloaded and installed to make your smartphone even *more* useful.

So you can use a smartphone to play games, write emails and browse websites. And you can reprogram them to do new things?
Exactly.

In that case, what's the difference between a smartphone and a computer?
That's a good question. For a while now, smartphones have been skating the thin line between 'fancy phone' and 'pocket computer'. Now, it seems, that line has disappeared altogether. Smartphones, essentially, *are* pocket personal computers. You've only got to peek inside one to see it. Just like a PC or notebook, inside a smartphone you'll find:

1) **Microprocessor chips**. These are similar to those used in most computers, only a bit smaller, simpler and less powerful. This helps to save battery power (and weight). As with larger computers, there is usually one core processing chip, plus a few extra ones to handle sound, graphics and video.
2) **Input devices**. While larger computers have a keyboard, mouse or touchpad, smartphones have fold/flip out keypads or high-sensitivity touchscreens. Where notebooks and PCs have webcams, most smartphones also have a high-resolution, digital camera built into them. This can function as a photo camera, a video camera or a webcam for video-calling. Plus, of course, all smartphones have built-in microphones for voice transmission and sound recording.
3) **Output devices**. Here, computer monitors and speakers are replaced with micro-speakers and small screen displays. In the future, smartphone output displays may be projected through **eyephones** instead, allowing the phones themselves to be made much smaller, and creating all kinds of new possibilities for augmented reality programs.*
4) **Operating systems**. Just as PCs and notebooks

---

* More about eyephones and augmented reality (AR) in the next questions.

use operating systems (OSs) such as Windows and OS X, smartphones have simpler mini-systems such as Android (for Google phones) and iOS (for iPhones). These provide a graphic user interface (GUI), and enable smartphone users (rather than just engineers) to reprogram their own devices using downloadable software 'apps'.

Aside from these main parts, many smartphones contain a host of other sensors – such as accelerometers and light sensors – that detect which way the phone is being held (upright or sideways) and automatically rotate photo and screen displays, or sense the light levels in the room, and adjust the screen brightness to compensate. Smartphone components and sensors are also used by apps in unique and surprising ways.

For example, with the translator app **Word Lens**, you can point your smartphone's video camera at a sign written in Spanish, and it will translate and display the text on the sign in English, as if by magic! And with the song finder app **Midomi**, you can point your smartphone's mic towards a radio or loudspeaker, and it will recognize the tune you're hearing and display it onscreen so that you can buy it. (To see my Top 5 list of handy apps – plus a few weird ones – see page 93).

So, if smartphones have turned into computers, won't they have to find a new name for them?

Maybe so. As smartphones continue to evolve, they get further and further from the traditional telephone, and we will almost certainly have to come up with another name for them eventually. The word 'phone' means 'sound' or 'voice'. Yet many smartphone users

hardly *talk* at all – they spend far more time texting, web-surfing, gaming, Facebooking and Twittering. But no one has yet managed to find a name that sticks.

How about 'smarty-box'? Or 'magical electro-thingy'?

Errr . . . yeah. We'll get back to you on that one . . .

Top 5 handiest smartphone apps

1. **My Homework** – organizes all your homework assignments on a calendar, and displays them in order of which one is due in first.
2. **Wikipanion** – basically Wikipedia in your pocket. Great for looking up people, places and historical events.
3. **Mensa Brain Test** – test (and retest) your IQ with a tricky collection of brain teasers.
4. **Word Lens** – translates English into Spanish and vice versa, just by pointing your phone's camera at it. More languages coming soon.
5. **StarWalk** – a pocket astronomy guide that helps you identify stars, planets, satellites, constellations (and space stations!) in the night sky.

. . . and the Top 5 strangest ones

1. **Pushups Dojo** – put your smartphone on the floor beneath you and do push-ups over it. This app will count how many. As long as you touch your nose to the screen every time, that is.
2. **Hang Time** – throw your phone up in the air, and this app will use its accelerometer to measure how long it was up there before you caught it. But if you *didn't* catch it you're gonna need a new phone.

3. **Hello, Cow** – just a picture of a cow. You touch it, and it goes 'moo'. Weird.
4. **Zits and Giggles** – squeeze virtual zits and boils onscreen, and giggle as the greasy white pus splatters across the screen. Nice.
5. **Pull My Finger/iFart** – two separate apps that serve the same essential function – annoying your teachers. They offer a range of realistic fart sounds, from 'trouser cough' to 'thermonuclear explosion'.

What will future phones be like?

Home telephones (or 'land-lines') will become a thing of the past, to be replaced by computers or home entertainment systems that make video calls. As for mobile phones, they will continue to shrink and develop new uses. One day soon, we could be 'wearing' these mini-computers invisibly in our clothing, and viewing the world through their digital eyes.

Wow. So in the future there will be no telephones?

Probably not. Not as we know them today, at least. Already, more and more people worldwide are using online calling systems like **Skype**, which let you place calls with a home computer. This is usually far cheaper than placing a phone call – especially over long distances – and, if webcams are available, you can make video calls to four or five people at once. In some places, you can also make video calls through an Internet-linked digital TV or games console. Eventually, it's likely that home computers, televisions, games consoles, and digital audio and video players will all be rolled into the same device, accessed via the same screen. When that happens, there will be no need for a separate telephone (or home stereo, satellite TV receiver, Blu-Ray player, and so on) device, and home telephone sets will be *history*.

So home phones will disappear? Like, completely? Maybe not completely. New technologies rarely replace older ones all at once, even when they're obviously much better. Take digital push-button telephones like the one you probably have at home, for example. They were first invented in the 1940s, and started turning up in homes from the 1960s onwards. Dialling with buttons proved to be much faster and easier than putting your finger in a rotating dial and cranking it round in circles.

In case you didn't realize it, this is where the phrase 'dial a number' comes from. In the old days, to place a phone call, you literally had to spin a dial to enter each digit. This took about two seconds per digit, so dialling a whole number could take twenty to thirty seconds. And *that's* if you didn't mess it up halfway through (which meant hanging up and starting all over again). With a push-button (or 'touch tone') telephone, it takes just five to ten seconds to enter the same number.

Man, what a pain! Who'd put up with that?

. . . and yet many people (especially older people) held on to their ancient, rotary-dial telephones for *decades* after push-button phones hit the scene.* Many just felt more comfortable with what they already knew, and were slow to accept those newfangled, push-button 'gadgets'. And that's probably how it will be again this time. Most people will ditch their home telephones in favour of cheaper, more convenient Internet video calls. But some will cling to their old-school phones for years.

Will most mobile phones become video-phones, too?

That's hard to say. In fact, many smartphones already contain video-calling technology, but people just don't seem to want to use it. That could be because holding the phone out in front of yourself (so that you can see the screen, and the camera can actually see you) is awkward and uncomfortable. Many people, perhaps, just don't *like* being seen while they talk. Besides, there's *far* more in store for the mobile phone than just turning them into portable video-phones.

---

* My parents still had one in 1987. To this day, I remember wrestling with it every time I wanted to call my best mate, Darren. 'Okay, so it's five . . . (wrrrrr, click) . . . eight . . . (wrrrrrr, click). . . eight . . . (wrrrr, click) . . . three – hold on . . . gahh! That should've been a nine! (click). Start again . . . five . . . (wrrrr, click) . . .'

Like what?

Many communication experts reckon that within a few decades, mobiles will shrink, disappear and turn into 'invisible computers' that help us manage our entire lives.

But how can they get any *smaller*? I mean, seriously – you can hardly hold on to the ones we have now. My dad can't see the screen on his without his glasses, and I'm always losing mine. My phone, that is. Not my glasses. Although I do lose those a lot, too . . .

That's true – mobile phones recently reached a point where they couldn't *get* much smaller, as the input devices (such as keypad buttons and touchscreens) and output devices (such as screen displays and speakers) would become too awkward to use. With separate headphones, earpieces and microphones you can talk and listen without having to hold your tiny phone up to your head. But how will you dial? And what about Web browsing and texting? Tiny keypad buttons are hard to press with chunky, human thumbs, and even people with perfect, 20/20 vision can't read letters less than a millimetre high. So this – so far – has put a limit on how small engineers could make handsets and screen displays.

But what if you had a flexible keypad on the sleeve of your jacket, or a digital screen display projected on the inside of your sunglasses?

That would be *awesome*. Could that really work?

Absolutely. Engineers are already experimenting with these new-generation input and output devices as we speak. They're building touch-sensitive 'smart patches' into clothes to create flexible (even washable) keypads. Some materials can even display digital images and video – like miniature, wearable movie projectors. With technologies like these, you could build smartphone components right into your clothing, turning your sweatshirt into an invisible, wearable computer.

Better yet, you could combine it with a set of tiny, wireless headphone and microphone 'patches' – stuck to your ear and throat or jawbone like tiny plasters to capture your voice and relay sound. Then you could add a pair of high-tech 'display shades', with a semi-transparent screen display visible only from the inside, so that you can see texts, webpages and YouTube clips right before your eyes. Some engineers are even working on eyephones – visual displays that are projected on to contact lenses, or even directly on to the retinas of your eyeballs!

Smart! Wait – that sounds a bit dodgy to me. Wouldn't that stop you from seeing where you were going?

Not necessarily. In theory, display shades and eyephones could **overlay** images and information on to the real world as you look at it. So you could follow virtual arrows to a Google-mapped destination, or look into shop windows and see the prices hovering above all the items. This is known as **augmented reality** (or **AR**), and many experts believe systems like this will become a part of everyday life in the near future.

So mobile handsets will disappear, too?

Maybe, or maybe not. As people start to call, text and retrieve information in different ways, mobile handsets will develop into something else – multipurpose digital controllers. One day, your mobile may function like an ID card, credit card, map, flash drive, house key, car key, TV remote control, all rolled into one. It'll become like a remote control for your entire life, working together with computers in your clothes, your home and your school, and making you the master of your own digital world.

Yeah! Digital *MASTER*. I like that. Can't wait . . .

3. Electro-tainment

How do remote controllers work (and why can't my grandad figure them out)?

Remote controllers work by beaming coded digital commands at your TV or DVD player, using pulses of light or radio waves. Some particularly nifty ones can be programmed to control several devices at once. As for your grandad – he didn't grow up with these fiddly gadgets like you did, so give him a hand.

My TV zapper sends *light beams* at the TV? How come you can't see them in the dark, then?
Because they're not beams of visible light. They're beams of infrared (or IR) light – a type of radiation that is invisible to the human eye.

Hang on – isn't infrared light a kind of heat? Like what comes out of those plug-in, electric heaters?
That depends on the type of IR radiation, or the **wavelength** of IR waves coming out of the device. We experience long-wavelength IR radiation (or 'far infrared') as heat. That's what comes out of infrared lamps and heaters. But remote controllers send out beams of short-wavelength IR (or 'near infrared') radiation instead. These do not feel warm at all,

and because our eyes can only pick up *even shorter* wavelengths of light (which we call visible light), IR is also invisible to us.*

So how do they work, then?

Basically, your average TV or DVD 'zapper' is a cross between an invisible torch and a code transmitter. It contains a small circuit board and processor – similar to those found in computers, only much simpler – plus a battery to supply power, and one or more light emitting diodes (LEDs) to produce flashes of IR light. When you press a button on the zapper (like '1', '2' or 'volume up'), the processor turns the command into binary** code, something like this:

1	00110001
2	00110010
Vol up	01110110 01101111 01101100 00100000 01110101 01110000

This done, the coded message is then beamed from

---

* But not to every animal on the planet. Many snakes – like rattlesnakes and pit vipers – can detect IR radiation with special sensory organs in their noses. So if you have a pet snake, then he (or she) may actually be able to 'see' the beams of IR shooting out of your TV remote controller. How cool is *that*?

** For more about how binary code works, see 'Do computers get angry or sad?', on page 24.

the LEDs in a series of short and long flashes, just like flashing Morse-code instructions from a torch. An IR receiver on the TV (DVD player, or whatever) then picks up the transmission, decodes the message and relays the instruction to a circuit or processor inside the device.

That's it?
Yep. That's it.

So why do remote controllers stop working sometimes?
How do you mean?

You know – like when you press the button, but nothing happens. So you have to wiggle the zapper around and press the button two or three more times before it changes the channel. I *hate* that.
That often happens when an object – like a chair, table or helpful pet – gets between the IR transmitter on the remote and the IR receiver panel on the TV. Even though it's invisible, IR light still travels in straight lines. So if there's something in the way, the message cannot get through. This problem usually gets worse as the remote battery wears down, making the light signal weaker. In this case, aiming the remote around the object (or just shoving the dog out of the way with your foot) should fix the problem. Another neat trick

is to bounce the IR beam off the walls or ceiling, by aiming the remote 45 degrees to the left, right or upwards. If, like me, you're easily amused, there's hours of fun in that.

Alternatively, you could buy a radio-frequency (or RF) remote controller instead. RF remotes work more of less the same way as IR ones, except that the coded, digital message is sent via radio waves, rather than IR light-flashes. Since radio waves can travel through many solid objects – even walls and ceilings – it won't matter which way you point the remote. Although if your neighbour has the same type of remote you may end up changing the channels on his TV instead. This can either be great fun, or grounds

for a fight, depending on how much of a sense of humour they (and your parents) have.

Ha! I'd like to try that. Okay – so why do we need so many different zappers? Like, one for the telly, one for the DVD, one for the satellite TV . . .
That's because each device (and each remote) uses its own set of codes to send and receive instructions.

But why? Why not just use the same ones?
Because the instructions to different devices might end up interfering with each other. Imagine how annoying it would be if every time you pushed 'play' on the DVD remote, it also switched off the TV. Or changed channels every time you turned up the volume.

Yeah, but it can get pretty annoying juggling three different zappers, too. Especially when my dad's always losing one of them down the sofa cushions.
That's true. To get around that problem, some fancy zappers, called **universal remote controllers** (or **URCs**), can be reprogrammed to control several different devices at once, by combining the **ID codes** and **command codes** from two or more separate remotes. ID codes are additional signals sent between remotes and host devices before the main **command codes** (like 'play' or 'volume up') are sent. It's a bit

like shouting 'Oy, telly!' or 'Oy, DVD!' before you give each command. In practice, a URC has extra buttons for each device. So, once you've reprogrammed it with the functions you need, you just press the button to select the correct device, followed by your main command. Then the URC sends one single stream of code towards your gadgets, which could be translated as:

'Oy, telly – BBC1!'

'Oy, DVD – pause!'

'Oy, satellite box – give us the menu!'

. . . and so on.

Of course, in the near future, we may be literally doing this – controlling our devices with our voices alone, rather than using buttons, codes and remotes. As voice-recognition technology improves, and begins turning up in more and more TVs and other gadgets, we will most likely end up controlling everything with our voices alone. Not just the telly, but room lights, temperature controls, ovens, toasters . . . you name it.

Seriously?!

Yep. In theory, you could come home from school,

flop into a chair and shout out, 'Telly on, lights off, movie channel 3, microwave on' . . . and in seconds you'd be enjoying your film with fresh popcorn toasting away in the microwave.

Yeah, but I can do that already. I just shout all that stuff at my mum.
Hmmmmm – but does that work?

Actually, not often, no . . .

How can you stuff 10,000 songs into one little pocket music player?

Because when songs are converted to mp3 audio tracks, thousands of tiny, barely-audible chunks are cut out of each sound file. This allows an entire CD's worth of information to be squeezed into ten to twelve times less digital space, and an entire music collection to fit almost weightlessly in your pocket.

What? You can get weightless mp3 players now? How does *that* work? Are they anti-gravity or something?

No, mp3 *players* aren't weightless. Small and light as they are, most still weigh a couple of grams, at least. But the mp3 files recorded on them *are* weightless. So it doesn't matter if your music collection totals ten songs, a hundred songs, or 10,000 songs – you can now get it all into one tiny device, and carry it around with you all day.

So we couldn't always do that?

Nope. No *way*. The technology for storing music like this only arrived within the last two

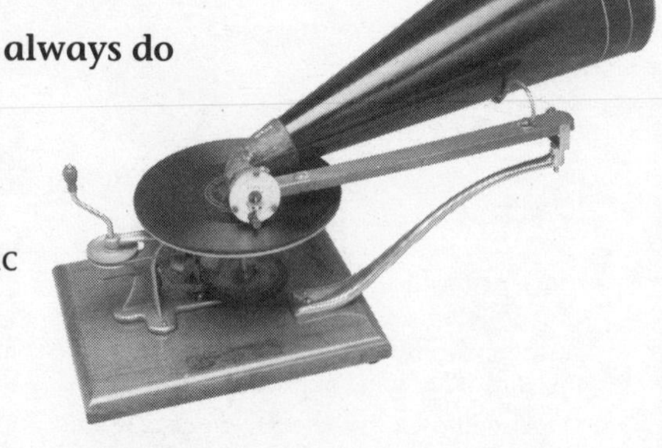

decades. Before that, recording and storing music was a much heavier problem. Literally.

Music recording and storage started out with American inventor Thomas Edison, who used a kind of microphone attached to a wobbling needle to scratch grooves into rotating wax cylinders. Later, these cylinders were replaced with large, flat plastic discs known to old folks and modern-day audiophiles* as '**vinyl records**', '**LPs**' (short for 'long playing records'), or simply '**records**'. Recordings were made in much the same way – with a needle carving a long, spiralling 'track' into each disc. To play them back, you would place them on a record player turntable.** This would spin as another needle (called the **stylus**) bounced up and down in the track and relayed vibrations to an amplifying horn, or to an electronic amplifier and speakers.

---

* An **audiophile** is someone who loves sound or music. The word is usually used to describe someone with an expensive home sound system, who hates mp3s and listens to music on records or CDs instead. Why, you ask? More about that in a minute.

** Also known in the early days as phonographs or gramophones.

Now each vinyl record held about ten to fifteen songs, so it would take about 1,000 of them to hold a full collection of 10,000 songs. With each record weighing 200 grams, that means your whole collection would weigh about 200 kg. Which is about the same weight as a fully grown polar bear. Imagine dragging *that* down the street.

Yikes! No thanks.
Exactly.

So what came next?
Next came **audio cassette tapes**, or simply '**tapes**'. With these, music was recorded magnetically on to long stretches of metallic ribbon or tape. The tape was then wound round two rotating spools and the whole lot housed inside a rugged plastic box. To play a tape, you placed it in a cassette player, which turned the spools and reeled the long tape over a magnetic **tape head**. The tape head picked up the magnetic 'tracks' in the tape and passed them to an amplifier and speaker. Tapes had the advantage of being smaller and tougher than records. Plus you could cram about twice as many songs on them. But they still weighed around 80 grams, and a 10,000-song collection

(crammed on to 500 tapes) would weigh 500 x 80 grams = 40 kg. Which would be like carrying your own bodyweight around in a massive backpack.

That's still no good, is it?

Nope. So next came **compact discs**, or CDs. CD burners turn sound information into binary code, and use lasers to burn the code into the surface of a mirrored disc, as a series of little dots and pits. A CD player then uses another laser to 'read' the code, converts it back into audible soundwaves and blasts it through an amplifier and loudspeaker. You could easily get your 10,000-song collection on to no more than 1,000 CDs. Since each one weighs just 15 grams, the whole lot would weigh 15 x 1,000 = 15 kg. About the weight of a big, heavy bag of potatoes.

After CDs came **minidiscs** (MDs), which didn't last very long.* This was rather sad, as although they

---

* At least not for music storage. MDs are still used to store computer data in some places.

weighed about the same as CDs they were about half the size, and had about five times the storage space of a CD. Spread across 200 minidiscs, your 10,000-song music collection would weigh 200 x 15g = 3kg. About the same as a bag of sugar. Which is not bad.

But it's not *great*, either.

Right. And the reason why MDs didn't last long? They were quickly replaced by mp3 files, which weighed nothing at all, and could be stored in their thousands in tiny mp3-playing devices.

But why? How?

Ahhh – that's all down to **digital compression**. Basically, when you convert digital music files (like those recorded on CDs) into mp3 files, a special computer program uses clever tricks to remove large chunks of the sound without us noticing.

So it removes whole verses or instruments? That doesn't sound so great . . .

No, not quite. It's a bit cleverer than that. Every sound recording, you see, contains a range of sounds we can't even hear, which are outside the range of

human hearing. By lopping those sounds off, the mp3-converting program saves a little space, and makes the audio file a little smaller (in terms of information, not song length!) Then it seeks out parts of the song where one instrument, singer or note is so much louder than the others that it drowns out all the rest. Since you can't really hear these background notes and sounds, anyway, the program happily removes those, too. Bingo – more space saved. Using tricks like this, an original recording can be cut down (or **compressed**) until it's ten to twelve times smaller, and you'll hardly hear the difference in the mp3 file that comes out at the other end.*

So how are the files stored inside the mp3 player – on tiny discs or something?

Some do that, yes. Hard-disk mp3 players (like the original iPod) have small **microdisk hard-drives** inside them, which whirr and spin away as they transfer and play back your music

---

* Unless, that is, you're an audiophile. With expensive music players and headphones, you'll easily tell the difference between the same song played back on a vinyl record, a CD and an mp3. Vinyl and CD recordings sound much 'fuller' and richer than mp3s. But most people don't know or care what they're missing, and use mp3s anyway.

files. These have lots of memory, and are great for storing entire music collections.

But most mp3 players around today are flash-memory players. Instead of moving parts and mini-hard-drives, they contain solid computer chips that store information much like the RAM memory* chips inside your home computer. While these can't hold as much information as a hard-drive, they're smaller, lighter and have fewer moving parts. So they allow flash-memory mp3 players to be built much smaller, or even placed inside smartphones. Thanks to compression, mp3s and flash drives, you can now store not just music, but also video clips and movies. This is what powers multipurpose smartphones and portable media players like the iPad.

Wow. I wonder what's coming next?

Who knows? But one thing's for sure – we've come a long way from wax cylinders and plastic records.

---

* For more about RAM and computer memory, see 'Do computers eat microchips' on page 15.

Will e-readers one day destroy books forever?

Maybe. But, then again, maybe not. There's no doubt that e-books and e-readers have already taken off, with millions already bought and sold across the globe. But although they may replace old-fashioned paperbacks in most places, the good ol' book is unlikely to disappear altogether.

Why's that, then? I mean, e-books are the new big thing, aren't they?

They really have exploded in popularity, yes. Especially over the last few years. In the US and Canada, a billion dollars' worth of e-books were bought by the end of 2010, and by 2015, that number will triple to at least $3 billion. E-book sales in the UK, Europe and Australia aren't far behind, and it won't be long before Asia and South America start to catch up.

But in the history of technology, one rule has been proved again and again – new technologies don't replace older ones just because they're *newer*. They replace them because they're *newer and better*.

But e-books *are* better than paper books!
Okay, if you say so. But think about it – in what *ways* are they better?

Well, for starters, they're lighter and easier to carry around.
Are they? While most e-reader devices are less bulky and heavy than hardback books (the ones with big, thick covers), they're not much easier to hold or carry than an average-sized paperback (thin-cover) books.

Yeah, but you can cram over a *thousand* e-books into an e-reader. What would a thousand paperbacks weigh?
Well, the average paperback weighs about 300–500 grams (8–10 oz). So a thousand of them could weigh up to 500 kg. In other words, about half a tonne.

Ha! Gotcha!
But then why would you want to carry 1,000 books around with you in the first place? Even on a month-long trip (about the amount of time it would take for an e-reader's battery to run out of charge), you'd have a job getting through more than ten or twelve

books. And what if your e-reader got lost, damaged or stolen? If you accidentally drop (or sit on, or spill lemonade upon) an old-fashioned paper book, it'll probably survive intact. But if you do the same to an e-reader, you could lose your entire library of e-books, all in one go.*

All right, then. How about this: e-books are better for the environment, as you don't have to chop down rainforests to make the paper. Boom!! Shazamm!! I win!!

Not necessarily. It's true, of course, that e-books don't require paper. But it does take an enormous amount of energy (not to mention water, plastic and rare metals) to build the e-reader devices you read them on. And unless that energy (and those materials) come from renewable sources then every e-reader built will use up limited resources, add extra carbon dioxide to the atmosphere and contribute to climate change.**

Of course, you can make books out of recycled paper, and make e-readers out of recycled materials, using renewable energy. But the point is neither type of book is perfect when it comes to the environment.

---

* Some e-readers and e-book services let you re-download books you've already bought for free. Others don't. And buying a thousand books all over again wouldn't be cheap . . .

** For more about how all this works, see my *marvellous* book on climate change, *Will Farts Destroy the Planet?*

Oh. Didn't think of it like that.
With all that said, there's no doubt that e-books are still becoming more and more popular with readers, and this trend is likely to continue. Over the next ten or twenty years, e-books will begin to replace paper books entirely in schools, universities and other places. With fewer and fewer paper books sold, old-style bookshops (as in, the ones you actually walk into) will start disappearing. Many traditional libraries will close down, too, as even the oldest books are scanned, turned into e-books and stored in vast, electronic 'e-libraries' containing billions of volumes.

So eventually *all* the old libraries will be gone?
Probably not, no.

Why? What good is a massive building full of books if you have e-copies of everything, anyway?
Well, for one thing, it would be smart to keep some of them around as 'hard-copy' backups. It takes a pretty serious fire to destroy an entire library building. But with millions of books stored in one digital memory bank a single computer-crash could wipe out thousands of years' worth of knowledge in seconds. Also, many people just *enjoy* the look and feel of paper books – they think of them like works of art, rather than just a collection of words and information. Think about it – just because we can

create digital photographs, designs and 3D graphics, doesn't mean we no longer look at oil paintings and sculptures in art galleries.

So even if e-books *do* offer many new advantages good ol' clunky, arty, paper books will be around for while yet. They've survived for centuries already, and they'll most likely survive a few more.

Hmmmm. I s'pose so. But will I still be reading them in the future, or will I go all 'e-books and e-readers'?

I guess there's a simple enough test for that: how are you reading this right now?

If you can download movies off the Internet, then what's the point in DVDs?

That's a very good question. Everything has to be stored somewhere, and DVDs are just one way of storing and ferrying video information. But their time will soon be up. With the rise of Internet movies, DVDs could soon be following dinosaurs and dodos into the sad, lonely dustbin of history.

Really? DVD movies are about to go extinct?
Not yet, but soon. Thanks to online movie libraries, they're definitely an endangered species.

What is a DVD, anyway? How do they work?
DVD stands for digital video disc. They were invented in the mid-1990s as a way of storing images, moving images (or video) and other types of digital information. Just like CDs, DVDs store information as a series of coded pits and dots, on the surface of a mirrored disc. Only instead of just sounds or music (audio data), the pits and dots on a DVD can also represent photographs, video clips or entire movies. Just as CD players use lasers to read and decode the audio information on a CD, DVD players use lasers to read and decode DVD video files. Converting images and video to and from binary code is a bit trickier than it is with sound. But

other than that, DVDs and CDs work in very similar ways.

So what's the difference between a DVD and a hard-disk drive? Is a hard-disk just a mini DVD player that fits inside a computer or iPod?

In some ways, yes. Inside, hard-disk drives (or HDDs) do look a bit like mini DVD players – complete with spinning disks and noisy, whirring motors. But unlike DVDs, HDDs do not use lasers to store and retrieve information, and aren't built to use more than one storage disk at a time. Instead, they use a tiny electromagnet on the end of a whirring arm to read and write information on a single disk or **platter**. The platter is usually made of aluminium, covered with a layer of magnetic material and it spins at up to 15,000 revolutions per minute (that's about five times faster than an aeroplane propeller!) as information is transferred back and forth.

But why do we need DVDs or HDDs, if we can just download stuff straight from the Internet instead?

Because, like I said, everything has to be stored somewhere. Even Internet movies. When you download an Internet movie or video clip, where do you think it comes from?

Err, I dunno. Someone else's computer?

Right. And how do you think the movie is stored inside that computer?

Ohhh, I get it. On a hard-disk drive, right?

Right. Or something like it. The Internet is a combination of information storage devices (like computers and servers) and delivery vehicles (like phone lines, broadband links, Wi-Fi transmitters). Without the vehicles, the information couldn't get about. But without storage devices like HDDs, there would be no information to shuttle about in the first place.

So CDs and DVDs are vehicles, now? Like cars, boats or aeroplanes?

Right. Only instead of safely 'storing' and shuttling passengers from place to place, CDs and DVDs store and shuttle information. They are the last in a long line of data-delivery vehicles that came before the Internet was powerful enough to store and shuttle information about for itself. And, just as Internet music downloads have begun to destroy music CDs, Internet video downloads will soon spell the end for the trusty DVD.

They will?

Yep. Almost certainly. Look at it this way – a few hundred years ago, the only way to enjoy music was to go to a live concert. Then clever types like Thomas Edison invented sound recording, and soon you could listen to music using 'music storage' devices like vinyl records, cassette tapes and CDs (which one you used depends on which decade you grew up in!). But then along came the Internet, and with it online music libraries like Napster, iTunes and Rhapsody. From 2004 onwards, music downloads began outselling CD sales every year, and more and more people are choosing to 'rent' digital music tracks from online libraries, rather than buy them one at a time.

Movies came later than music, but they're following the same path. Just fifty years ago, your only option for watching movies was to go to a 'live screening' at a cinema. Then video cassettes were invented, and by the mid 1980s, millions of people were taking movies home in their boxy, plastic 'video storage' vehicles. After video cassettes came DVDs (and, since then, HD discs and Blu-Ray discs). But, now movies can be downloaded or streamed over the Internet, fewer and fewer people are buying DVDs each year.

The point is, once the Internet came along, we didn't need to store and shuttle our music and movies around in records, tapes, discs or other 'vehicles' any more. The Internet does both – it *is* the music and movie library, and it *is* the vehicle for getting them about.

So I s'pose I should just recycle all my DVDs, then? Not much point in keeping them now . . .

Well, you might want to keep your rare ones and favourites, just as backups (just in case they get erased

from the iTunes library or something). Plus you might enjoy looking back at them one day, remembering what it was like 'back in the old days'.

Like what my grandad does when he breaks out his suitcase of old, blurry photographs?
Exactly. Imagine – one day you could be boring your own grandkids with *Avatar* or *Harry Potter* on DVD . . .

Puzzle: Music and Movies Crossword

Across

1. Buzz___________ – astronaut star of 8 across (9).
4. Device that can hold over 10,000 electronic books (1,6).
7. What the 'H' in 'HDD' stands for (4).
8. Animated film about a group of talking toys (3,5).
9. 3D movie about a planet inhabited by blue-skinned aliens called the Na'vii (6).
11. American engineer who invented the first music-recording device (6).
12. Cowboy star of 8 across (5).

Down

2. Book and movie series about a powerful boy-wizard (5,6).

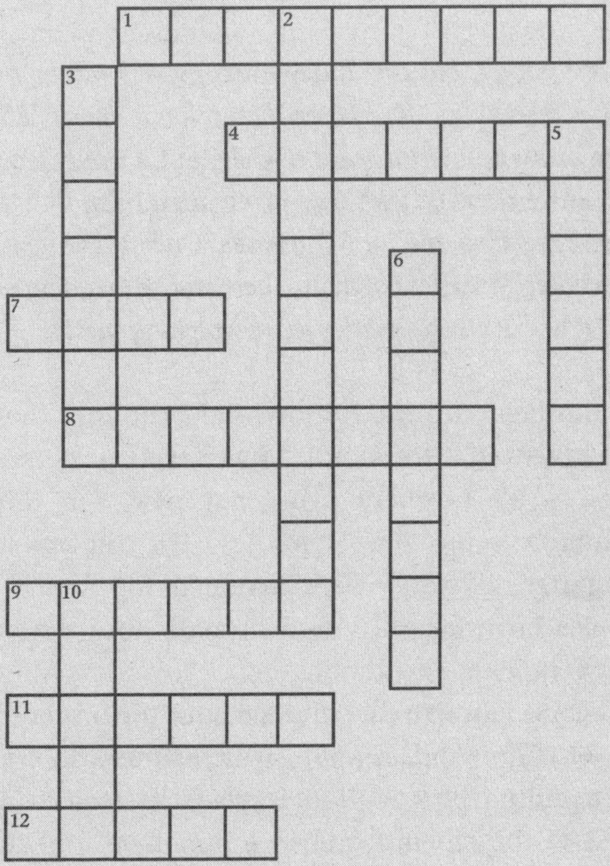

3. What the 'C' in 'CD' stands for (7).
5. Vinyl disc used to record and play music (6).
6. Type of invisible light used in TV remote controllers (8).
10. What the 'D' in 'DVD' stands for (5).

(Answers on page 229.)

Will all future movies be in 3D?

Maybe not all, but eventually **most** *movies will be made and screened in 3D. Three-dimensional movie effects have been around for quite a while. But it's only recently that we've come up with ways of creating them that don't involve wearing special 3D glasses. Once these new '3D screen' technologies catch on, there will be no going back. And it won't just be movies we're watching in 3D.*

3D has been around for a while? I thought they just invented it for *Avatar* or something . . .

Nope – it's nowhere near that new, I'm afraid. Although some new types of 3D camera (and computer software) were invented for *Avatar*, 3D movies have actually been around since the early 1900s. In 1903, the famous French inventors Auguste and Louis Lumière shot and screened the first ever 3D movie (*L'Arrivée d'un train*), which simply showed a train pulling into a station. It proved so 'realistic' that most of the cinema audience screamed and dived for cover behind their chairs. In the 1920s, more filmmakers began experimenting with 3D films, but the idea never really took off.

Later, in the 1950s, 3D briefly became very popular in the USA as film studios began making horror films and monster movies in three-dimensional 'terror-vision'. But the eye-straining 3D glasses moviegoers were forced to wear to watch the films created more

headaches than screams. So, before long, people went off them. Since then, developments in movie technology have led to better and better 3D efforts (including high-resolution 3D IMAX movies). But it was only in the last few years that engineers figured out how to create 3D effects *without* the use of those uncomfortable (and pretty silly-looking) glasses.

How does 3D work, then?

There are lots of different ways of creating a 3D effect. But all of them rely on **stereoscopic vision,** and fooling the brain into thinking **two separate 2D images** are actually **one single 3D image**.

Some of the earliest 3D movies were made using different-coloured 2D images and lenses. Basically, you take two pictures (or two film clips) from two slightly different angles, then tint them different colours (usually one red, one green). This creates a pair of analyph images, which you then project (using separate projectors) on to the same screen. To create the 3D effect, the viewer must put on a pair of coloured glasses with tinted lenses (again, usually one red, one green). The lenses block one image from getting to each eye, so that one movie 'angle' enters each eyeball. Your brain mashes the two angles together, and is fooled into thinking you're looking at a real 3D scene (rather than flat images on a flat screen). The effect isn't great, but it's easy to create. In fact, you can even make analyph 3D pics (and glasses) for yourself (see page 134).

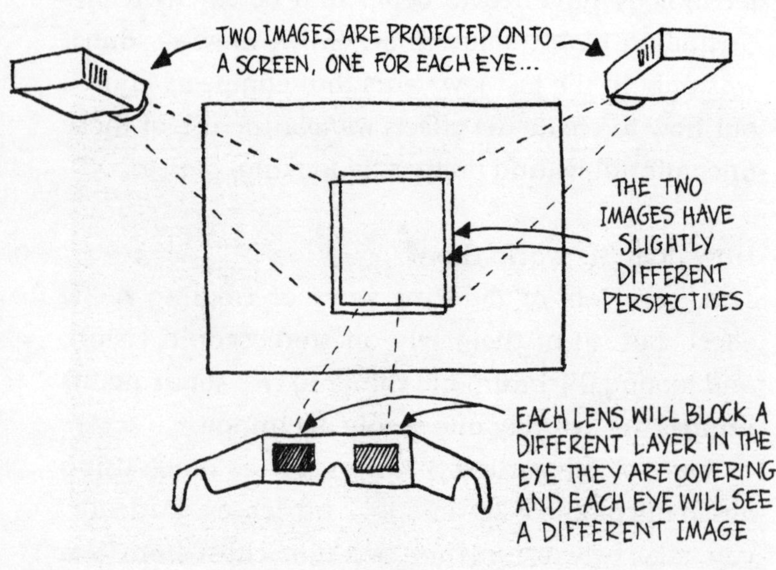

Different-coloured eyeballs? That's pretty crazy.

Right. This is what gave all those 1950s moviegoers headaches. But thankfully that wasn't the end of the story.

After coloured glasses came **polarized 3D glasses** and movies. With these, you film the same scene from two slightly different angles, as before. But, instead of tinting the images two different colours, you project them with two separate projectors, each one with a different **light-polarizing filter**. These change the patterns of the light waves coming through them, so that – when you view them through glasses with **polarizing lenses** – only one image reaches each eyeball. Again, your brain assembles the inputs from each eye and is fooled into thinking you're looking at one three-dimensional scene. Polarizing 3D is the kind of technology currently used in most cinemas

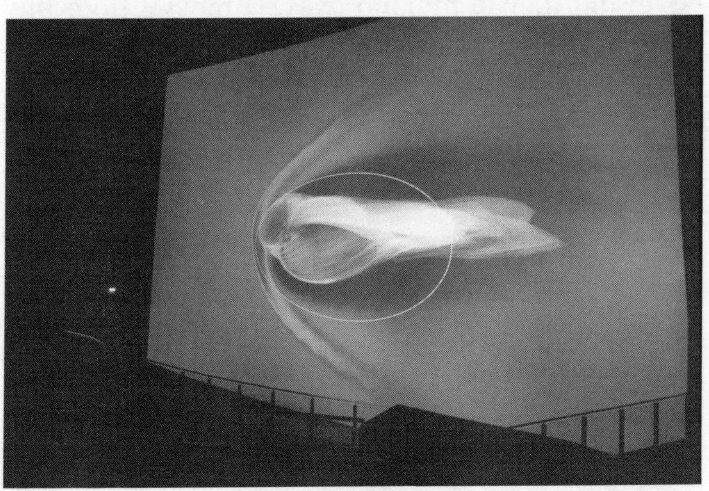

(including 3D IMAX theatres), and the kind used to make movies like *Avatar* so realistic.

So does that mean they'll make more and more 3D movies now, instead of 2D ones?

Well, for now 2D films still far outnumber 3D ones. But as the technology gets better and better we'll probably start getting bored of 2D, the way your grandparents eventually got bored of movies without colour, and your great-great-grandparents got bored of movies without sound. Sure, there are still some silent movies and black-and-white movies around. But they're rare. Movies are about escaping into an alternate reality – so the more realistic that reality looks, the better. Already, some of the world's biggest movie directors like James Cameron (who made *Avatar*), George Lucas (who made the *Star Wars* films) have said they're making *only* 3D movies from this point on. As have animation studios like Dreamworks (who made *Monsters vs Aliens* and *How To Train Your Dragon**). So it looks like the future of movies will be gloriously three-dimensional.

What about 3DTVs? Will they be everywhere, too?

Eventually, yes. But 3DTVs are a bit different, and have taken a bit longer to come around. You can't use

* Which happens to be one of my favourite films of all time. See it! Best. Movie. Ever.

the two separate projectors with a TV display, so you can't get away with using the same polarizing filters and glasses. For a long time, this created a problem. But recently TV makers have come up with a couple of solutions.

The first was to use **shutter glasses**, which have liquid crystal display (LCD) lenses that black out one eye at a time, flicking 'on' and 'off' about 120 times per second. In short, your 3DTV flicks back and forth between two separate-angled film images, and your LCD, eye-masking glasses sync up with it, allowing only one film angle to enter each eye. This works, but dims the overall image, making the screen look 3D, but a little dark.

That's not much cop, is it?

Perhaps the best solution is only now starting to hit the shops. With **Parallax Barrier 3DTVs**, all the 3D-creating trickery occurs on the screen, and there's no need to wear glasses at all. Instead, a grid-like screen in front of the main TV screen (called a **parallax barrier**) flips between two different shapes, allowing light through at different angles at different times. Again, this ensures only one set of images reaches each eye, which creates a 3D image effect in the brain. Some 3DTVs have permanent parallax screens (so 3D is 'always on'), while others have LCD parallax screens that can be switched off. This makes the flickering parallax barrier transparent, and returns the TV to ordinary 2D.

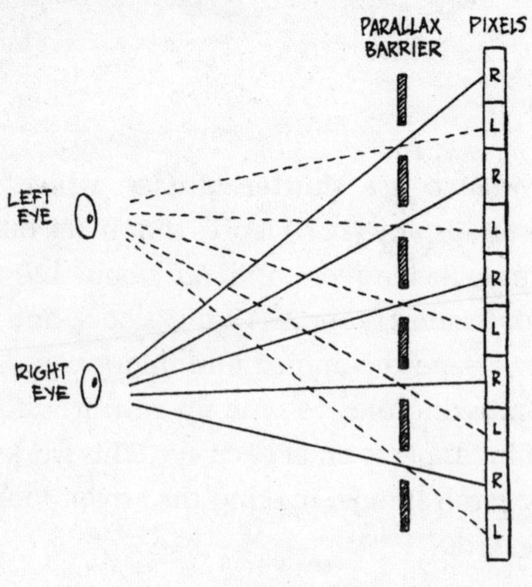

The effect still isn't perfect. But because we can see these 3D screens without special glasses we can now put them on **anything with a screen**. So, pretty soon, you can expect 3D screens to turn up not only in cinemas and home televisions, but also on everything from PCs and laptops to tablets, cameras, camcorders, smartphones and handheld games consoles. Soon, you'll be making your own 3D movie clips, browsing 3D web pages and playing 3D games on the bus.

Brilliant! When do we start?
Soon. Very soooooon . . .

Activity: make your own 3D glasses!

Want to create your own 3D images and view them in the comfort of your own home? Follow these simple steps, and let the 3D eye-boggling begin.

1) Go to a local joke or toy shop, and buy a pair of plastic glasses with frames but no lenses. Alternatively, you can ask a family member if they have an old pair of sunglasses they want to get rid of, and carefully press the lenses out. Or you can make your own out of cardboard (measure your face and the distance between your eyes first, so that they fit properly).
2) Now find an art shop, and ask for two small sheets of coloured, semi-transparent acetate plastic – one red, and one blue.
3) At home, place the glasses on the red acetate paper, draw round the left eyepiece, cut out the shape you just drew, stick it to the glasses (making a coloured left lens) using sellotape. Now place the glasses on the blue paper, draw round the right eyepiece, and repeat for the right side. You should now have a pair of 3D glasses with a red left lens and a blue right lens.
4) Now go to http://www.3d-image.net/gallery.php, and use your glasses to view the 3D images on the page. You can also download free 3D-image-making software from this page, and make your own 3D pictures. Enjoy!

What will future videogames be like?

Future videogames will be spectacular to look at, mirroring real-life scenes in eye-popping 3D. So realistic, in fact, that it'll be hard to tell whether you're watching someone play a game, or watching a ***real*** *race, battle or sporting event on TV. There will also be many more types of games, more people playing together online, and more people playing games in general. Some gamers may even spend most of their time living and working in a virtual, global 'game-world'.*

G-g-g-g– . . . what? . . . that's . . . can I . . . uhhhhh . . .
Eh? What's the matter?

There's so much *brilliance* and *coolness* going on in what you just said that I don't know where to begin . . .
Okay. Just take a breath. Relax.

Whew! Okay. I'm fine now. So . . . even more people will be playing games in the future?
Yep – certainly looks that way. As videogames and gaming consoles develop, improve and become cheaper to buy, more and more people are playing them worldwide every year. As of 2008, around **10 million** PS3 consoles, **17 million** Xboxes and

21 million Wiis had been sold across the globe. By 2010, that rose to **42 million** PS3s, **45 million** Xboxes and **76 million** Wiis. A third of all families in the UK own a games console of some kind. In the USA, it's more like half. And the videogaming explosion shows no sign of slowing down. In the future, many gaming systems will be built right into home TVs to make all-in-one **digital entertainment systems**. When that happens, it's a fairly safe bet that there will be a games system in almost *every* home in the developed world, just as TVs are found in most homes now.

All right! So what will the actual games be like?

As the power and graphics of computers and consoles continue to improve, games will become incredible to look at, and unbelievably realistic to play. Driving games will have cars racing on tracks and city

streets rendered in amazing, real-life detail, perhaps merging with systems like Google Maps to show real buildings, landmarks and road signs flashing by. Flight simulators will depict aeroplanes and airports in *exact*, super-realistic detail, and players will fly through rain and snowstorms updated in real-time by online weather services. If it's raining outside, it'll be raining in your game.

Will they be 3D, too?

The move to 3D gaming has already begun. At the moment, 3D games are fairly basic, and you have to wear special glasses to get the effect.* But as 3D screen technology improves and spreads it'll start to appear in almost every game available and, before long, old-school 2D games will be a thing of the past.

As game **control interfaces** get better, old-school **game controllers** will probably start to disappear, too. Right now, most games are still being played with handheld gamepads, with buttons you attack with your fingers and thumbs. But already movement-sensing **motion controllers** – like those found on the Wii and Xbox Kinect – are becoming popular with gamers worldwide. Eventually, devices like this will probably take over completely, and almost *all* games will be controlled with natural, whole-body

---

* For more about 3D glasses and screens, see 'Will all future movies be in 3D?' on page 126.

movements. Whether you're driving, shooting or fighting off ninjas with your awesome kung-fu skills, it'll be done with minimal props (like perhaps a pair of gloves and a frisbee-like steering wheel) and a lot of moving your hands and feet through empty space.

Sweeeeeet.

What's more, game props like gloves, guns and steering wheels will start to give realistic feedback as you race or battle your way through a game. With special **thermal** and **haptic feedback** devices, electronically triggered heat and pressure pads lining gloves and handgrips will make your hands vibrate or feel hot as you wrestle with the wheel of a skidding race car, push back against your palms as you pick up objects and let you feel the thwacking impact on your fist as you thump an unfortunate ninja. Some games may even feature whole haptic bodysuits that – when combined with 3D displays or eyephones* – will

---

* For more about eyephones, see 'What will future phones be like?' on page 95.

create seamless virtual reality (VR) worlds that you can not only **see** and **hear**, but also **touch** and **feel**.

This just gets better and better! So you'll be right *inside* the game, and it'll look just like real life?
Well, maybe not exactly like real life. Creating complete, photo-realistic VR worlds would take more computing power than most consoles are likely to have for a long, long time. But the goal of VR isn't to recreate the real world perfectly – it's just to make the game feel *real enough* to fool your brain. With the right gear, you can do that without photo-perfect graphics.

VR and natural motion controllers also allow **more different types** of games to be created, and more **uses** to be found for games besides just 'play'.

Like what?
Like training games that teach you how to ride a motorbike, sail a yacht, fix a car engine or build a house. Trainee doctors can learn how to do operations with virtual scalpels and organs. Trainee policemen could learn how to search for clues in virtual crime scenes. The list is almost endless. One day, games like this will probably become a part of school lessons and college courses. Imagine if your homework tonight was 'play virtual surgeon and complete level 3: heart transplant'.

You mean play games for homework? *Now* you're talking.

It could happen, and *soon*. In the future, people won't just be playing with videogames, many will also be *working* with them. In online, Internet-linked games like *World of Warcraft*, players already form groups, work together, design outfits, buildings and furniture, and trade clothing and other items for real money. In the future, videogames will merge with social networking systems like Facebook to create **virtual workplaces and businesses**. Virtual 'game-worlds' will contain real shops and services, with real people working in them all day long. Virtual game characters from opposite sides of the globe will meet, talk and trade real-world goods and services in Internet game-world locations. And they'll get paid to do it.

Ha! I *knew* it! My mum's always telling me to lay off the videogames cos they're a waste of time. But if I'll be playing games for a living then what's the point in homework and school?
Well, if you want to actually *get* that videogame job, you'll still have to do your schoolwork so you can learn about how computers and businesses work, and how to work in teams with other people (whether they're in the real world or virtual world). For that, you'll need to know your maths, science and English. And if you work with virtual team-mates from across the world, you'll still need to learn their languages, their cultures and the countries they come from. For that, you'll some knowledge of foreign languages, geography and history. And, if you don't want to turn into a pale, wheezing blob sitting in front of a computer screen, you'll still need to get outside and play real sports and games to stay healthy.

(Sigh.) Okaaaay. A bit of homework, some footy outside and then it's back to some serious gaming, okay? After all, it's for my *future*, right?
Better ask your mum – that one's not up to me!

4.
E-worlds and Interwebz

Who built the Internet?

No one person or country built the Internet. It began with an experimental computer network designed by the American military. But the World Wide Web we use today was built over three decades, by millions of people, in countries all over the world.

What? The Internet was a military experiment?

Sort of, yes. In 1969, the United States military's Advanced Research Projects Agency (or ARPA) designed a network of computers that spanned three American states (California, Nevada and Utah) and covered a distance of over 2,000 miles. They called it ARPANET. It wasn't the Internet, but it was an Internet.

What do you mean by that?

Well, ARPANET was the first practical, long-distance, **Inter**-communicating **Net**work* of computers. And while it isn't the same network we use today (ARPANET was shut down in 1990, by which time today's Internet

---

* That's how today's Internet eventually got its name: 'Inter-Network' became 'Inter-Net' . . . geddit?

had grown to replace it), it was perhaps the first working 'internet' the world had ever seen.

So what did they build it for? Was it so generals could email orders to soldiers all across the world, like, really quickly?

Errr, no. It wouldn't have been much use for that. When it was first built, ARPANET only linked together four places. Three of these places (Los Angeles, Santa Barbara and Palo Alto) were in California, and the fourth (Salt Lake City) was in the state of Utah. And since all of these places are in the western United States, ARPANET wouldn't have been much use for emailing military orders across the globe.

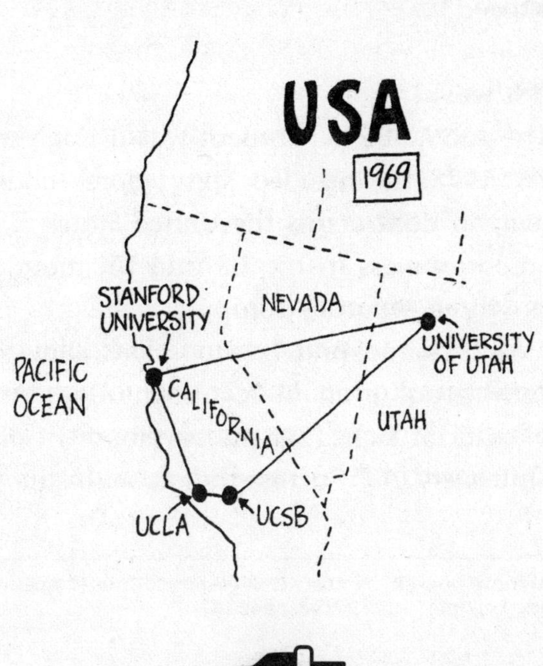

What was in those places, then? Was it top-secret military bases, where they hide huge nuclear missiles or alien spacecraft or something?

No, nothing that exciting, I'm afraid. These four places were all sites of American universities with high-tech electronics laboratories. ARPANET was designed as an experiment – to see if it was possible to send, receive and store information across an interconnected network of computers. The idea was to share information between 'nodes' (or clusters of computers) located hundreds of miles away from each other. That way, research information could be easily shared across long distances, and would be kept safe even if one or more computers were stolen or destroyed.*

So did it work?

Yep. The ARPANET experiment was a huge success, and by 1975, it included sixty more 'nodes', in cities spread right across the United States. Then in 1977 programmers in the US and UK managed to link up three separate computer networks in San Francisco, Virginia and London. This showed that an international (even intercontinental) internet was possible, and it kicked off the development of other 'mini-internets' right across the globe. In the 1980s,

---

* Or later on 'hacked' by nasty (but clever) computer spies or 'hackers'.

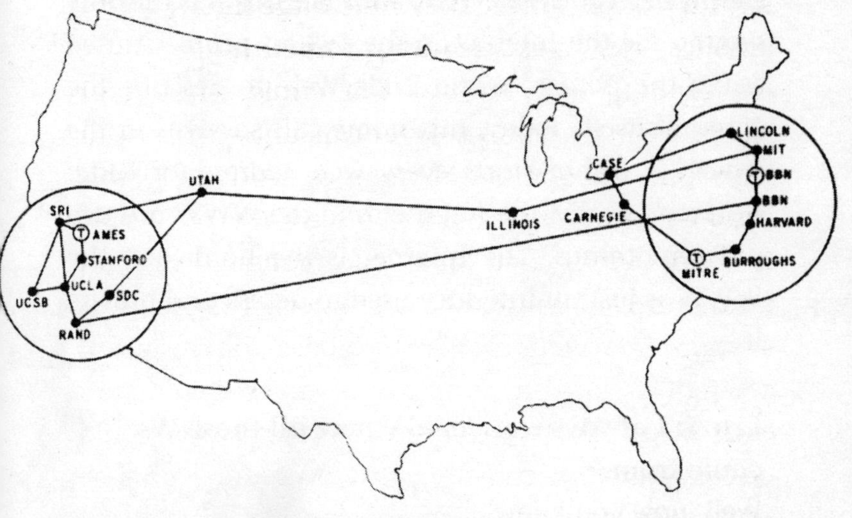

internets sprang up in Europe (CERNET), Australia (AARNET) and Japan (JUNET). By the end of the decade, these had been linked up with a growing American network (not ARPANET, but a new, non-military network designed to replace it) to form a truly global network.

So then it got all linked up, and they renamed it the World Wide Web?

Not quite. That name came about kind of by accident. In 1991, British engineer and programmer Tim Berners-Lee invented the first internet browsing program, which eventually allowed every computer on the internet to 'see' every other. He called his program 'WorldWideWeb', but since this was the only way to see the Internet in the 1990s,* people started using the phrase 'World Wide Web' to describe the Internet itself. Today, this name still survives in the 'www . . .' that starts every web address (or URL). But, technically, the Internet and the WWW are two different things. The Internet is the hardware; the WWW is just an interface used to access and browse it.

Crazy. I always wondered where all those Ws came from.

Well, now you know.

So what actually is the Internet? I mean, where does it live, and what is it made of?

The Internet now lives all over the world, spread out between millions of 'nodes' worldwide. It's basically made of three things:

1) **Information** – this includes words, numbers, images, sounds, music, video clips, web pages and raw computer data or code.
2) **Information hosts** – these include desktops, laptops, tablet computers, mobile phones,

---

* Today, there are lots of browsers programs, including Microsoft Internet Explorer, Mozilla Firefox, Google Chrome and more. But back then WorldWideWeb was pretty much it.

memory drives, computer servers and anything else hooked up to the Internet that can be used to store information.

3) **The global telecommunications network** – including modems, routers, telephone lines, fibre-optic cables, satellites, microwave transmitters and more. Basically, everything that's used to shift information between information hosts.

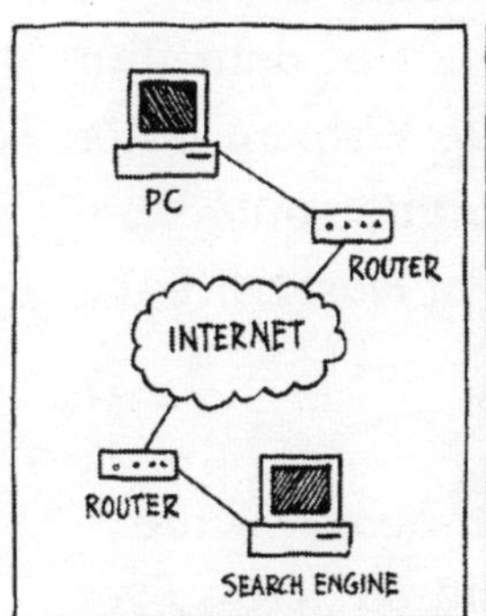

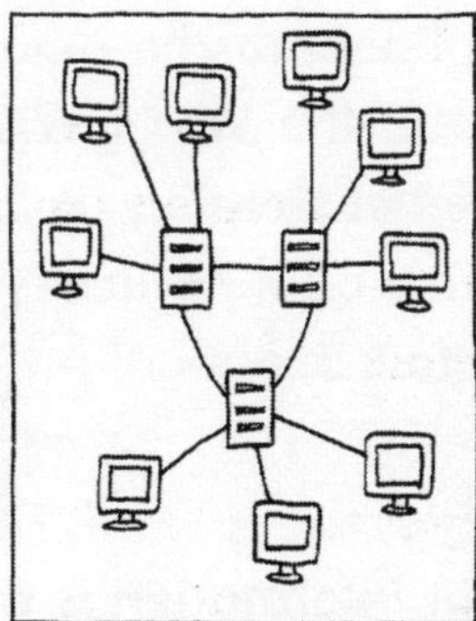

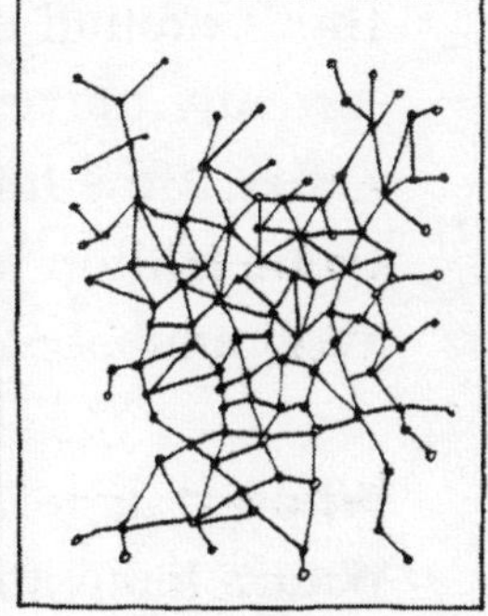

That little lot – all connected together to the brains and fingers of Internet users worldwide – is what makes today's Internet the vast, powerful virtual information monster it is today.

Whoa. Sounds pretty big.
It is. In fact, it's hard to fathom just how big it has become.

Go on, then – how big?
That all depends how you measure it . . .

In terms of people or users, the Internet now includes around **1.8 billion** people worldwide. That's roughly a **quarter** of the population of the entire world.*

In terms of information, the Internet now contains over 5 million terabytes of computer data. To give you an idea of how much that is, the first iPods could store 5 gigabytes' worth of music, which – if you owned one – gave you 'over 1,000 songs in your pocket'. That's around a billionth the amount of data that currently makes up the World Wide Web. In other words, if the Internet were an iPod, you could store over a **trillion** tunes on it. Which is at least twice the total number of stars in our galaxy.

Whoa . . .

What's more, that information is shared across over **150 million** websites (and over a **trillion** individual web pages) worldwide.

Seriously? A trillion web pages? So how long would it take to read them all?

If you read one per minute – without ever stopping to eat, sleep or go to the toilet – it would take round about **31,000 years**. Coincidentally, this is roughly

---

* Although these users aren't spread out very evenly. In the UK and USA for example, roughly two-thirds of the population are on the Internet – 40 million people in the UK, and 220 million in the USA. But in Africa, South America and South-east Asia, less than a tenth of the population is similarly 'hooked up'.

also the age of the entire *Homo sapiens* species. So if you printed out every page on the Internet, crammed it into a time machine and travelled back to give it to the first ever human . . . then his descendents would still be trying to finish it now.

Actually, I think it'd take a bit longer than that.
Why's that?

Well, for starters, cavemen couldn't actually read, right?
Ah. Good point.

Why do all web addresses start with 'http'?

Actually, not all of them do. Some start with 'ftp', 'smtp' or other letters instead. But 'http' is the most common address-starter because it stands for **hyper-text transfer protocol** *– the original (and still the most popular) way of pinging information back and forth across the Internet.*

Okay, so I get the 'www' bit in web addresses – that just stands for World Wide Web, right?
Right.

So what's the difference between the Web and the Internet?
The **Internet** is the hardware, or the 'nuts and bolts'. It's the sum total of all the machines, wires and wireless links that form the backbone of our super-handy, global computer network. The **World Wide Web** (or **Web**, for short), is the software, or the information. It's the sum total of all the interlinked documents, pictures, video clips and data packets that are stored, sent and received via the Internet.

Well, that's a bit confusing. Why didn't they call them something different? I mean, a net is hardly much different to a web, is it?
Fair point. I'll be sure to take that up with the whole world tomorrow.

You do that. Okay – now I get why the 'www' turns up in so many web addresses. But what does that 'http' bit stand for, again?
Hyper-text transfer protocol.

Hyper-text-what, now?
Hyper-text transfer protocol is the Internet's main **networking protocol**. In other words, it's a way for computers in a **network** to **request information** from one another, and to **respond** by sending back the information requested.

Basically, http is what keeps all the documents, pictures and pages of the Web linked together. And it's how Web information gets transferred (or routed) between those who **have** it, and those who **want** it.

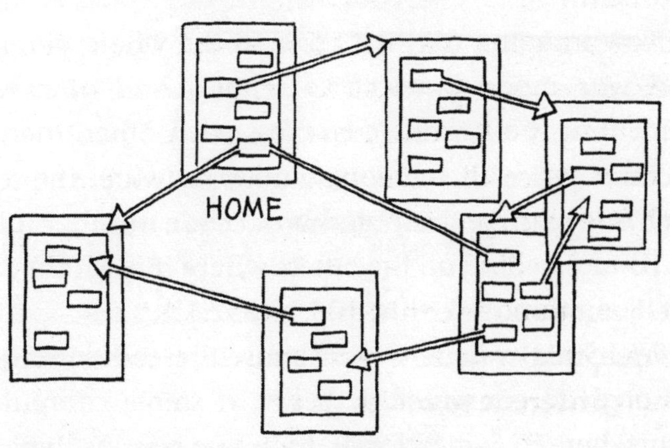

But I thought you just typed in an address, or clicked a link, and your computer went to the page you wanted automatically.

Well, if you think about it, your computer doesn't really **go** anywhere, does it? It just sits there. It's the information that moves. When you click a link, the information on a web page **travels to** your computer – not the other way around.

Okay, your computer *grabs* it, then.

Nope. That's not quite how it works either.

So what *does* happen when you click a web link?

Here's how it works:

Imagine a huge net. Literally. Like the net in a football goal, with criss-crossing strands that join up to make squares or diamond shapes in the spaces in between.

Now imagine that net covered the whole planet, and was made of electrical cable. And at every point that the strands criss-cross each other, there's a computer, with memory banks, software, the lot. Each one of these computers has a **code number** (like an ID tag), telling all the others **where it is** within the net. Something like this: 103.13.252.1

With this system, if you know the code number for a given computer (let's say, a single computer somewhere in Switzerland), then you can just type it into the web browser of **any** computer, **anywhere** on the net, and it'll send a request to the Swiss computer for information. In response, the Swiss computer pings back a file list (or index) of what it has to offer, and you look at the list and go from there.

Now in real life it's a little more complicated than that. While you can connect to other computers if you know their computer 'ID' codes, your computer does not (and could not) contain a list of every other computer, everywhere in the world. Instead, your computer knows one handy ID number – that of your local internet service's main **server** – which it uses to find and contact the others.

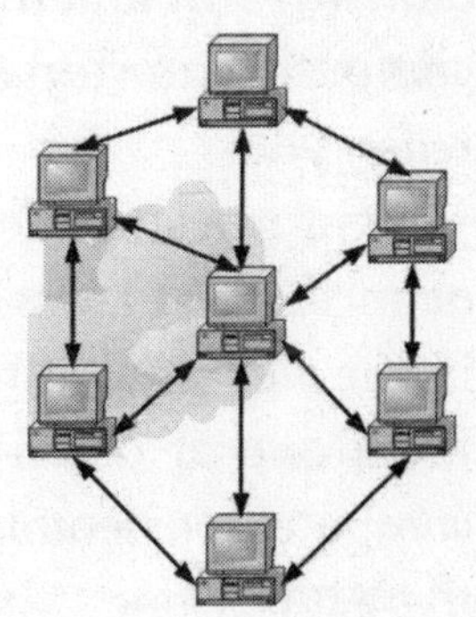

Now the local server is like a popular big brother with a thousand Facebook friends. It doesn't have all the other computer's ID numbers, but through all the computers it 'knows', it does know quite a few. When you click a link or type in a URL, your computer pings its popular big brother with a request to hook up with one of his friends – a friend *your* computer doesn't know yet, but one who owns (or simply holds) the web information you want. In turn, the big-brother server passes that request on to all his computer 'mates', and they spread the word through the net that someone is looking for 'that

Swiss guy with the funny cat pictures'.

Eventually, a connection is made, the Swiss computer is pinged with a request for information and it responds by pinging a message back through the extended network of computer 'friends', until it reaches your computer again. Now the info-pathway through the net has been opened, the Swiss computer can start sending web pages through it to reach you.

In practice, whole web pages are too big to send all at once. So the Swiss computer breaks the information in the web page into lots of little packets and sends them one at a time. Then, at the other end, your computer reassembles them like a jigsaw puzzle. And there it is. Done.

That's it?

That's it.

So how come you never see those ID numbers kicking about? I mean, after the 'http://' and 'www.' bits, it's all words, not numbers.

Ah, that's just because words are easier to remember and tell apart than numbers. Every word in a web address actually hides a number, and the whole web address (or link) eventually gets turned into a number as it's pinged back and forth between web servers and 'computer friends' in the network.

Of course, if you *do* know the numbers, then

you can use those instead. But, personally, I find http://www.glennmurphybooks.com a lot easier to remember than http://104.209.521.1 . . .*

* This is not the correct ID number for the GlennMurphyBooks server. I just made it up. So please don't try it, as you might end up in the MI5 computer or something by mistake.

Internet Word Search

```
H G P X R K Q K V S B N U K B Z K A K
B R O W S E R H O F A E W P J S T J W
P I I O L A T E E P B O W W N Q U H X
A Q X I G D Q U S I S B O S E S C U Z
X P N P I L R A O Q A R I N E D O A N
Z K M M Z T E O Z R L T I R L R O Y O
E W E B S I T E R D X Q V I Q W N N T
A E R Q F W H G W E R E J N O E U S S
R B B C V X F I T Q R I L G T W W W O
P P W T L B D R K V P X N W G W A G H
A A Y J F E E T C Q Y Y O U T U B E T
N G U U W P V I N F O R M A T I O N T
E E Y E Y S Y V D E K S R M H R F R P
T D B H G O P C Y K O O B E C A F U O
```

ARPANET	browser	Facebook
Google	host	HTTP
hyper-text	information	link
network	node	router
server	webpage	website
WorldWideWeb	WWW	YouTube

(Answers on page 230.)

Why do computer screens have windows?

Clickable windows and icons create a handy way to navigate computer files. That said, not all computers have them. Two-dimensional 'window' interfaces are very common in home computers, but there are other interface systems out there. These range from dull-looking lines of coded text to complex, three-dimensional displays. In fact, if you really know your computer stuff, you'll soon discover that windows are just for WIMPs.

Oy! Hang on a minute – are you calling me a wimp?
What? No, I didn't . . .

Yes, you did. You said windows were for wimps. Well, my computer has windows. So that means I must be a wimp, right?
No, no, no – I said **WIMP**, not *wimp*.

What's the difference?
A wimp is a nasty name for a weak or cowardly person. But **WIMP** stands for **w**indows, **i**cons, **m**enus, **p**ointer. It describes the key parts of the interface system you'll find on most PCs and laptops. A system in which a **pointer** (a cursor moved around by a mouse or touchpad) is used to select **icons** (little pictures that represent files or programs) that are

conveniently arranged into **windows** and **menus**.

The WIMP structure is the backbone of Windows™, Mac OS X™ and other visual computer interfaces. Computer programmers would call this type of 'look, point and click' system a **graphic user interface** (or **GUI**, for short*). So, like I said, windows are for WIMPs.

Oh. I see. All right, then. I'll let you off.

Thank you.

But don't all computers have those GUI things?

Not all of them, no. Before GUIs came along, most computers were controlled and explored with simple text commands. GUIs were first invented in the 1970s, but their trusty windows and icons were rarely seen on computer screens before the release of the Apple Macintosh (or Apple Mac) computer in 1984. Before that, computer users had to navigate files and programs manually, by typing out coded instructions.

When you powered up an old-school, pre-1980s home computer, you weren't greeted with a Windows or Mac desktop. You'd just see a blank screen,

---

* This is pronounced 'gooey'. Which leads immediately to this popular computer programmer joke:

> 'Hey – is your interface all GUI?'
> 'Why, yes – it is.'
> 'Well, wipe it off, then! LOLOLOLOLOLOL.'

(Sigh.) It's funny to them, I guess.

and a little flashing dot or line. This was called a **command prompt**, and it prompted you to enter new instructions – to search for a document, to load or run a program, to log off the system – as coded text.

If you want to get a feel for what this was like, you can try it on your home computer – even if it has a GUI system (like Windows) installed. To do this, turn on your computer, log in as usual and then go to Accessories>Command Prompt. You'll see a little black window, and a C:\ followed by a flashing line. Congratulations – you're now free to enjoy controlling your computer without having to click icons, menus or windows. Provided you know the code words, of course. Try a few of these:

To do *this* . . .	**. . . enter *this* phrase**
Open the control panel	control [enter]
Open the calculator	calc [enter]
Open the Paint application	mspaint [enter]
Log off	logoff [enter]

Hey – it works!

Of course it does! Even today, this is the *only* way to control a *brand new* computer before its GUI software (Windows, OS X, or whatever) is installed. And, as a matter of fact, many expert computer users choose

never to install a GUI. They shun windows and icons altogether, because they feel that GUIs use up too much memory and slow their computers down.* Instead, they 'keep it old-school'. They run programs, alter settings, open documents and play music and video files with simple text commands.

Hardcore computer programmers, in particular, rarely bother with windows and icons. They spend so much time typing commands and running applications that it becomes almost a hassle to them to start clicking through windows for their files.

So they don't use a mouse or touchpad at all?

Well, many still happily use **menu-based interfaces** – lines of text arranged in drop-down lists that you can select with a mouse or touchscreen cursor. These menu-based interfaces came before GUIs, and you can still see them at work in mobile phones, mp3 players and other gadgets with screens too small to make windows and icons useful. But most things are controlled with a few rapid clicks of the keyboard.

So what's the point in having windows at all, if you can control your computer without them?

For starters, GUIs allow computer users to access

---

* This is true. They do. At any given time, a lovely-looking GUI like *Windows 7* – and the services that go with it – might be hogging up to half of your computer's total processing power. Which doesn't leave much for other programs . . .

programs and files visually, which is helpful for novice computer users or typists,* and they're a nice alternative for arty, visual types who simply *prefer* pointing and clicking to typing. GUIs also allow you to avoid typing repetitive commands (programmers don't mind this so much, since they do this all day anyway, but *you* might). And they can be handy for switching quickly between related tasks – like writing an essay in one window, while Googling facts for it in a separate web-browser). So while programmers may shun their windows and icons, the rest of us mere mortals find it difficult to live without them. Since the release of the Windows 3.0 program in 1990, the use of GUI systems has *exploded* in home PCs and laptops. Nowadays, it's hard to find a shop-bought home computer without one.

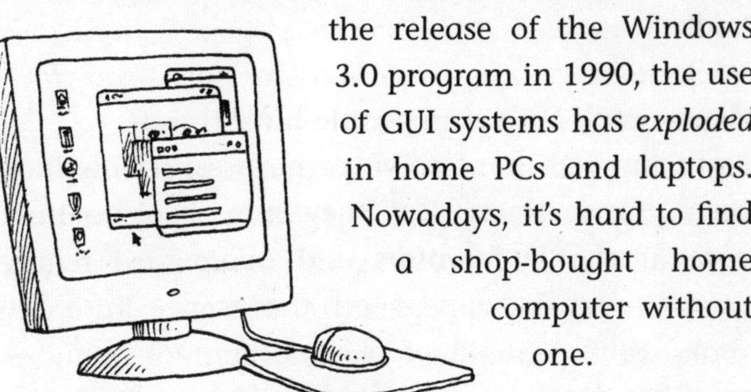

So are there any other types of interface out there, besides GUIs and typed-in text commands?

Yep – quite a few. Some advanced computer operators use sophisticated three-dimensional (3D)

* If you've ever seen your elderly relatives hunting and pecking away at the letters on a keyboard – taking a full twenty minutes to write a short email message – then you'll know who I'm talking about.

user interfaces instead. These include many mathematicians, scientists, engineers and graphic artists. 3D interfaces are especially handy for building 3D graphs from complex scientific data. Engineers use them to create 3D models of buildings, vehicles and gadgets before they set about building the real thing, as part of the computer-assisted design (or CAD) process. Computer artists may use them to help with 3D artworks and computer-generated movie effects. And programmers may use them in the creation of 3D gaming experiences and virtual reality (VR) simulations for pilots and soldiers.

Wow – cool! Do many people have those?

Right now, outside of a few specific uses, 3D interfaces aren't so common. But they may become more popular as 3D monitors and augmented reality* display systems appear on the scene. In a few years' time, instead of clicking through windows on a flat monitor, we may be looking at 3D 'boxes' projected directly on to our glasses, contact lenses or eyeballs. Combine that with physical interface devices (much like those seen with the Wii or Xbox Kinetic today), and you'd have a whole new way of exploring your computer. Just think – you could

---

* For more about these, see 'What makes smartphones so smart?', on page 87.

scroll through spinning 'box' files with a flick of your hand, open an Internet browser with a quick nod of the head and send an email with the blink of an eye.

Yeah, but you'd look pretty weird doing all that in public . . .

How does Google search the web so quickly?

It doesn't. Computer programs like Google, Yahoo! and Bing are essential for finding online information. But if they searched the entire Internet for it, you'd still be waiting for an answer ***years*** *from now. Instead, they look through a kind of 'Internet Index' put together by robots called 'spiders', 'ants' or 'crawlers'.*

You're having me on. That's not right.
What's not right?

Seriously? I'm supposed to believe that Google is run by an army of robot ants and spiders?
Well, ants and spiders don't actually *run* Google. (Some very, very rich people do that). But they do *work for* Google. What's more, Google couldn't work *without* them.

Look, if you don't know the answer to my question, you can just say so . . .
I'm serious! It's true! Of course, they're not real robotic spiders and insects. The Internet is a virtual,

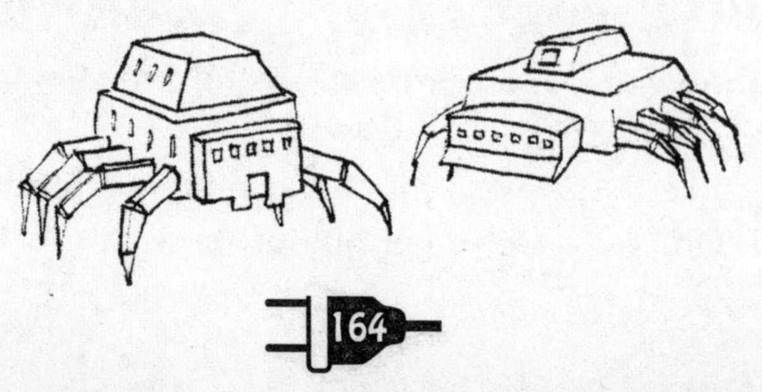

electronic library, so it takes virtual, electronic robots to crawl through it and gather information. These so-called 'web crawlers' are actually computer programs, designed for that very purpose.

But why would you need them at all? I mean, Google is a computer program, right?

Right. Google is an example of a **search engine** – a computer program designed to find information for you on the Web. There are many search engine programs out there, but only a few are used worldwide, and none are used as widely as Google. Other popular search engines include **Yahoo!**, **Bing** and **Ask.com**. But none of these programs actually searches the whole Internet when you type in a word, phrase or question.

They don't? Why not?

Because, quite simply, there's *way* too much information out there, and it'd take *way* too long to do it. Look at it this way – if you had to find out, say, who ruled Egypt during its fourth dynasty, from 2589 to 2566 BC. And you weren't allowed to use the Internet. What would you do?

I dunno. Go to the library or something. Ask for a book about Egypt.

Okay. Let's say you got there, and the librarian said 'Oh, yes – we've got one of those. It's in here

somewhere. Feel free to look around. What then? Would you search through the thousands and thousands of books on the shelves, flicking through each one in turn to see if there's a mention of Egypt or pharaohs? Even if you ignored any books without 'Egypt' in the title, it would still take ages to find the right books, and *even longer* to flick through them for a rare mention of its fourth-dynasty ruler.

Don't be stupid. Nobody would do it like that.
So what *would* you do?

I'd ask the librarian where to look.
But how does he or she know where to look?

They've got an index or something. A big list of which books they have, what they're about and where you can find them. Then you follow those funny numbers on the shelves till you find the right one.
Exactly! Large libraries use an **index** or **central database** system to keep track of what's on their shelves. Without this, even the best librarian in the world couldn't hope to find the right book (and the right page) among thousands of possible choices. And so it is with the Web.

As you've already learned,* the World Wide Web

* If you haven't, see 'Who built the Internet?' on page 142 for details.

contains over a *trillion* pages of information, and it would take over 31,000 years for a person to read it all. Even the most powerful search program would take at least a year or two to search every word, on every page of the Web, every time you asked it something. So, rather than waste years of your time, search engines such as Google act like virtual librarians. Instead of searching the whole Web for the information you need, they look it up in a huge, central Web database – an index to the library of Internet information.

So who made the index?

Ahh, you see – *that's* where the robot spiders come in. Automated 'web crawler' programs (also known as ants, or spiders) scour the Web day in, day out, reading virtual labels (called meta-tags) attached to billions of web pages which tell them what the page (or site) is supposed to be about. They then compile lists of web page addresses or (URLs) along with a list of key words that describe each page. So a web page about the history of Egypt, for example, might have a list of meta-tags (or keywords) like this:

[Egypt; history; pharaoh; Nile; pyramids; Ramses; Tutenkhamun . . .]

. . . and so on. A web-crawler program scans (and rescans, since web information can change every

day) thousands of web pages this way, and adds the addresses and keywords it finds to a central database. *This*, then, becomes the library index that a search engine like Google will flick through when you type in a word or search term.

So that's how search engines get the answers back so fast?
Right.

Because the robot ants and spiders have already done all the searching and indexing for them?
Right. Plus people (usually web-page designers) will add to the index themselves, by *sending* addresses, meta-tags, keywords and other information about their websites to Google and other search engine companies. This helps Google build their database faster, and helps the website owner to get their website found.

Okay – I think I get it all, now. There's just one more thing that's bothering me. . .

Who *did* rule Egypt from 2589 to 2566 BC?
Ahh, you'll have to find that out for yourself . . .*

* Oh, all right then. Turn to page 230.

Game: Speed-Googling!

Search engines like Google are a great way of finding information on the Internet. But sifting through all the results to find the information you really need can be tough work, and is a skill in itself. Grab a friend and test your Googling abilities with this quiz.

Here's how you do it. You need a computer with two browser windows open – one open at www.Google.com, the other at www.e.ggtimer.com. On the e.ggtimer window, type in '5 minutes' into the box to set the countdown. Now grab a piece of paper and a pen, and write the numbers 1–20 down one side. When you're ready to begin, click 'GO!' on the e.ggtimer, flick back to the Google window tab and quickly find as many answers as you can to the questions given below before the time runs out. Write the answers down on a piece of paper.

For even more fun, try racing a friend! There are two ways to do this: if you have two computers, you can sit side by side, count 3–2–1 and start your e.ggtimers at the same time. If you only have one computer between you, then have one person leave the room (so they don't see the answers the other finds) and go one at a time.

Ready? Set? *Google!*

1) What is the capital of Kyrgyzstan?
2) On which day does Japan's 'Umi no hi' ('Ocean Day') fall?

3) Name the four US presidents carved into the famous Mount Rushmore.
4) Who was Great Britain's first prime minister?
5) How many of Greece's 6,000 islands are inhabited?
6) What is the atomic number of the element Einsteinium?
7) A female deer is called a doe; what is a female bear called?
8) How tall is the Eiffel Tower?
9) Which ancient Greek author wrote *The Odyssey* and *The Iliad*?
10) In which year did we last see Halley's Comet?
11) When can we expect to see Halley's Comet again?
12) Who built India's famous Taj Mahal?
13) Name the two moons of Mars.
14) Mount Everest is the highest mountain in the world. What is the second highest?
15) What is the official language of the Philippines?
16) Which famous sculptor created *The Thinker*?
17) In terms of land area, what are the world's three largest countries?
18) King Henry VIII had six wives. Which two did he have executed?
19) Which famous composer and violinist wrote *The Four Seasons*?
20) Where do I live?

Who delivers my emails?

Actually, ***no one*** *does. With* ***billions*** *of emails being sent every day, there's no time or space for real people in the global, electronic-mailing system. Your emails are sorted, routed, stored and delivered automatically by Internet-linked computers and email handling programs. And, unlike human postmen, these incredible e-posties deliver your mail at over 300* ***million*** *miles per hour!*

Let me get this straight – *no one* delivers my emails? No one at all?
Nope. No posties, no couriers, no people at all.

How do the messages know where to go, then? And how do they *get* there?
Well, let's start with this – how does normal mail (or 'snail-mail') get to where it's going?

Easy. You just stick it in an envelope, scribble an address on the front and lob it in a postbox. Then the postie does the rest.
So the postie picks up your letter from the postbox, reads the address and carries it straight there in his van?

Yeah. Something like that.
But what if you send a message overseas, to some remote corner of Siberia or something? Does the

postman spend weeks travelling there and back, asking for directions along way? Maybe his van gets stuck in the snow, and he has to trade it in for a sled and a team of husky dogs . . .

All right, all right. Maybe it's not *that* easy . . .
Exactly. There are actually quite a few steps involved in getting your letter where it needs to go. And before we start talking about how emails get about it's important to understand how mail works in general.

So how does it work, then?
Here's the deal . . .

- First, you **write your message**, shove it in an envelope and **write two things** on it: 1) the **name and address of the person it's going to**, and 2) the **name and address of the person it's from.***
- Next, you take it to the post office** and get it stamped and **postmarked with the time (or date) you sent it**. This done, it's **sorted into a pile** based

* In the UK, where I grew up, you can get away with leaving this bit out. But in the USA, where I live now, the posties won't take a letter unless you put the sender's name and address on it, too. Since email works more like the American postal system, we'll say you need both things on the envelope for the purposes of our story.

** Either that or you put a stamp on and stick it in a postbox. This adds an extra step, but the end result is the same – your letter gets picked up by a postie, ends up getting sorted at a post office sorting centre somewhere, where it sits in another pile waiting to be picked up *again*.

on the general destination, and it sits there with a pile of other letters mailed at the same time until a postie comes to pick the whole lot up.

- After that, your letter gets transferred to an appropriate **vehicle**, and is driven/shipped/flown to the general area in which the receiver lives. There, it arrives at a local sorting centre and gets sorted into yet **another pile** based on the local address.
- Next, a local postie picks up his 'local' pile, heads out on his rounds, and drops the letter off at the receiver's address. This might be a house letterbox, a central letterbox serving a whole block of flats, or (if you have one) a rented P.O. box* in a local post office.
- Finally, someone at your receiver's address picks up the letter from their **postbox** (or, possibly, off the doormat) and bingo – your letter has arrived.

Wow. That seems like a lot of steps for one little letter.

Maybe now you can see why it takes days or weeks to send and receive regular mail. The pickup, sorting, transporting and delivering all take time for people to do. This adds up, and makes it impossible to deliver a

---

* Lots of businesses have these, to keep their business mail separate from their personal mail. Which is why you see things like 'P.O. Box 125' instead of house numbers and street names on business addresses.

letter (at least through a general mail system) in less than a day.

Email, on the other hand, is sent and received in seconds, because the sorting is done at super-speed by computers, and the transporting and delivering is done by moving digital information 'packages' through networked wires and waves at blinding speed. Here's how an email gets sent:

- Using an **email program** on your computer (like *Gmail* or *Outlook*), you **write your email message**. This message includes the **names** and **electronic addresses** of the person it's going **TO** and also the person it's **FROM**.
- When you click 'SEND', the email program **'postmarks' the message** with the **current time and date**, and sends it through an Internet connection to an **email server**. This is just an Internet-linked machine with an email handling program installed. The server then **sorts** your message into a **electronic 'outgoing' pile**, which is immediately handed back into the Internet.
- The high-speed Internet now becomes your mail's delivery **vehicle**, as it speeds through fibre-optic cables and wireless networks to reach an **incoming mail server** closer to the receiver's real-world address. There, it gets **sorted** into an **incoming mail pile** and stored until the receiver is ready to check their email.

- Whenever the receiver gets around to checking their email, they fire up **their** computer's **email program**, which contacts the incoming mail server through the Internet, and retrieves the whole store of messages held in the server's **electronic P.O. box** (or **Inbox**)
- Finally, the receiver clicks on the message title, which downloads the message from the server to their **computer's Inbox** and bingo – email delivered.

The whole process from SENDing to arriving in the server's INBOX takes less than half a second, which is around three times faster than you can blink. This means that if the email travelled from the UK to Australia, then it did so at over **306 million miles per hour**, or close to half the speed of light.

Whoa. That's one seriously speedy postie.
Yep. You said it . . .

Quick Email Quiz

Test your e-knowledge with this quick multiple-choice quiz. Guess a, b or c for each question, then go to page 230 to see how you did.

1) Roughly how many emails are sent, worldwide, every day?
   a) 1 million
   b) 10 billion
   c) 100 billion

2) How much of this is spam?
   a) about 10%
   b) about 50%
   c) about 90%

3) Which country sends the most spam messages per day?
   a) India
   b) USA
   c) Nigeria

4) When was the first ever email sent?
   a) 1972
   b) 1982
   c) 1992

5) Who was the first head of state to send an email?
   a) The president of the United States
   b) The prime minister of the United Kingdom
   c) The queen

Will e-lessons replace schools one day?

Partly, yes. But not entirely. Future lessons will have to change in order to keep up with a fast-changing world, and online, 'virtual' learning will eventually replace old-style classrooms and textbooks. But schools won't disappear altogether. Instead, they will become something much more interesting and fun – an all-day learning centre for everyone to enjoy.

Enjoy? We are talking about *school* here, right?
Yes, we are.

But school is B-O-R-I-N-G.
Oh, come on – it can't be that bad. There must be *some* things about going to school that you like.

Well, I like seeing my friends, and playing games. And some classes and projects are okay, I s'pose.
So what don't you like?

Pretty much everything else, really. Getting up early, getting into trouble when I'm late. Remembering which books to take, and lugging them from class to class. Being stuck in boring classes I'm not interested in, and missing the chance to get out and do stuff. All that.
Ah, but much of that could change in schooldays of

the future. You see, most schools around today have stayed pretty much the same for the last hundred years. National schools were first created to prepare kids for working in the nineteenth or twentieth century. For the most part, that meant working in factories or offices.

Back then, factory and office workers were expected to get up early, travel to a central workplace and start work on time every day. Each day, working hours, lunch hours and break times were controlled by clocks and watchful supervisors. Late and absent workers cost these businesses money, so anyone caught not working (or not where they were supposed to be) would be punished. And once they were *at* work most workers weren't expected to solve problems, make suggestions or be creative. They just had to show up, do what they were told, work a full day and repeat the whole cycle for years on end.

So to prepare kids for this experience, schools were set up with basically the same features. School students, it was decided, should get up early and arrive on time – 'clocking in' (or sitting in registrations) at the workplace to make sure they weren't late. After that, their days of study would follow strict timetables, controlled by school clocks, bells or chimes. Get up, go to school, do what you're told, go home, repeat. Sound familiar?

Ugh. Sadly, yes. But will future schools really be any different?

If they want to prepare kids for modern working life, then they'll have to be.

In the twenty-first century (at least, for most people in developed countries), work is now a very different experience. Thanks to advances in technology, fewer and fewer people are working in factories and office buildings, and more and more people are working from home, via the Internet. Co-workers can be spread across the globe, using email, instant messaging and webcams to communicate and work together. They no longer have to be in the same room to 'meet' and discuss the project they are working on. With a laptop, a webcam and a Wi-Fi connection, they can talk to anyone, anywhere in the world – without ever having to leave their homes. So, if students want to be prepared for all this, then future learning will have to change to reflect it.

You mean we'll do schoolwork from home, and meet with classmates online instead?

That'll be part of it, yes. There will still be subjects to study, and things that have to be learned – like maths, English, languages, arts and sciences. But each student will have their own personal course of study, specially designed (with the help of a tutor or computer program) to meet their interests and goals. Instead of working from textbooks

in classrooms, students will be emailed learning assignments, projects and challenges by subject tutors, and expected to complete them in their own way.

Some tasks you might work on alone – researching facts and figures online, working through learning software or visiting real museums, zoos or science labs to find out more. For other tasks, you might have to work with others – creating blogs and webgroups with classmates, and meeting up (online and in person) to chat, gather information, carry out surveys and experiments, observe wildlife, take pictures, build things, write stories and create web pages and slideshows.

That sounds brilliant! But what about teachers? Won't we need them any more?

Students will still need tutors, yes. But their roles will change from 'givers of information' to 'expert learning guides'. Instead of standing in school classrooms all day, tutors (like students) will spend much of their time interacting with students online – assigning tasks, answering questions, meeting with project groups and reviewing the products of completed 'coursework', such as web pages and online documents. Some tutors will be full-time 'teachers', while others might be professional scientists, engineers, artists, athletes and businesspeople, who offer part of their time as learning assistants. Some

tutors might even be computer programs or robots – specifically programmed to help students explore key subjects.

Cool! So we won't have to go to school *at all*, then? Will they knock all the old schools down?
No, many or most schools will stay standing – they'll just be *used* differently. In addition to all the e-lessons and online stuff, there are still good reasons for having a place for students to meet, work and play together. After all, you learn a lot more from going to school than how to do sums, write essays or speak French.

You do?
Yep. You also learn how to interact with others (in person, not just online), how to make friends, how to sort out differences with people, how to play fair in sports and games, how to sing, dance, paint, draw, sculpt, play musical instruments and more. To help with this, school buildings will be altered and adapted, becoming more like local community centres. Stuffy halls and classrooms will be replaced with open lounges, workshops, laboratories, meeting rooms with big, round tables, and wide open spaces for playing sports, planting gardens or whatever.

Gone will be the pencils, pens and notebooks – instead, everyone will carry laptops, touchpads or tablet computers. The school will be open all day

and all night, and students will come and go as they need to. School ID cards will carry computer chips that automatically log the students in and out of school, so that teachers and parents can track their movements when they're away from home (and check that they're still studying, rather than just at the movies or on the beach!). The same cards can be swiped through sensors to get access to computer rooms, pop open your locker, or buy a meal or snack using topped-up money credits. Students and people from the local community will meet there to play sports, stage performances, jam in rock bands and more. All in all, it'll be a pretty exciting place to be.

Wow! If my school was like that, I wouldn't mind going there at all!

Well, just hang in there – the future might come round quicker than you think . . .

5.
Androids and A.I.

How clever is the world's cleverest robot?

Not very, I'm afraid. Despite all you may have seen in the movies, the robots aren't anywhere near bright enough to take over the world just yet. In the latter half of this century, we may see the first truly 'clever' robots emerge. But for now even the world's most advanced robots are less agile – and far less intelligent – than most dogs, monkeys and toddlers.

Hang on – that can't be right.
Why do you say that?

I saw a robot on YouTube walking, talking and climbing stairs like a real person. You're telling me that's not clever?
Well, that all depends on what you mean by 'clever'. The robot you saw on YouTube was probably Honda's ASIMO robot (or something like it) – a walking, talking, humanoid robot designed to mimic human movements and actions. There's no doubt that a lot of clever people put a lot of work into making ASIMO. To see him move, respond to voices and recognize faces is certainly very impressive, and ASIMO is definitely a major step towards building smart, humanlike

robots. But is ASIMO *himself* really all that *clever*? Most engineers and scientists would say no.

That seems a bit mean. Why's that, then?

If you look up 'clever' in a dictionary, you get something like this:

Clever (*adjective*)

1. Nimble or dexterous with the hands or body.
2. Displaying sharp intelligence.
3. Mentally bright, quick or original.
4. Sly or cunning.

Now by *any* of those definitions, it's hard to call ASIMO – or other modern-day humanoid robots – clever.

Let's take the first one, for example. While ASIMO can walk (and even jog) at low speeds, he can't skip,

leap, roll, tumble, crawl, peel a banana or climb a ladder using his hands. That makes him considerably less nimble than most monkeys and toddlers.

As for 'sharp intelligence' or being 'bright, quick or original', ASIMO can be programmed to recognize specific **faces**, but cannot recognize simple **facial expressions** like happy smiles and angry frowns. He can recognize specific words and phrases, but cannot tell the difference between a happy giggle and an angry shout. He can be programmed to perform a sequence of dance steps, but will not learn to move for himself by copying the movements of others. In fact, ASIMO can't do *anything* he isn't specifically programmed to do beforehand. That makes him less intelligent than most pet dogs. And as for 'sly' or 'cunning' – well, let's just say that ASIMO will *never* try to sneak a sausage off your breakfast plate, or cheat at a game of cards. He just doesn't know how.

But I saw another one that could play the violin. Like, *really* play the violin. I can't play the violin. Doesn't that make it cleverer than me?

No, it doesn't. Again, that violin-playing robot might *look* clever, but it can't do anything it's not specifically programmed to do. The tune it's playing – complicated as it is – is simply stored in its memory as a sequence of movements. It has no idea what the notes are, what the tune should sound like. If you ask it to play something else – anything else – it simply cannot, unless someone spends hours programming the movements first. And, if you grab the violin out of its hands, it'll just stand there, twiddling its fingers in space, playing 'air-violin' until someone tells it to stop.

Oh. I never thought of it like that.

From an engineer's or scientist's viewpoint, humanoid robots like ASIMO aren't very 'clever' at all. For engineers, the 'cleverest' (or most impressive) robots are those that are both nimble (or **dexterous**) and **useful**. After all, a robot that can play the violin is fun to look at, but what good is it?

When asked to name a clever robot, robotics experts will usually point to complex assembly or handling robots used in car manufacturing or heavy industry. The most advanced ones have *more* freedom of movement than a human arm or hand, and can switch tools *by themselves* so that at one time a hand is a welder, another a cutter, another a grabber and so on. While it's perhaps no more 'intelligent' than humanoid robots like ASIMO, it can do things human

workers can't do, and can practically put together an entire car by itself. It's hard to say that's not clever, by comparison.

What about those chess-playing robots that beat human chess champions, or those online chatbots that fool you into thinking they're real people? You're telling me they're not clever, either?

Well, for starters, they're not really robots (*'bots* for short). Deep Blue – the 'chessbot' that beat grand-master Garry Kasparov in 1997 – wasn't a robot, it was a computer. (There was no puzzled-looking android sitting opposite Kasparov at the table. The computer would analyse the board and come up with new moves, then a *person* would make the actual moves on the board). And online 'chatbots' like

Chomsky aren't robots, either. They're just computer programs – just lines and lines of computer code stored away in a machine somewhere, and accessed via the Internet.

In both cases, there is little real intelligence or 'cleverness' going on. Chess computers just crunch numbers to predict their opponent's likely moves from the millions of possibilities on the board, while chatbots simply draw their answers to human questions from thousands of responses that have been pre-programmed by humans.*

Similarly, interactive learning robots like the **i-Que** toy ('the World's Smartest Robot') have memory chips containing entire dictionaries and encyclopedias, and can recite hundreds of thousands of facts and definitions. But there's a big difference between **information** and **knowledge**, and an even bigger difference between **knowledge** and **intelligence**. To be knowledgeable, you need more than just lots of information. You need to be able to relate bits of information to each other in meaningful ways, and understand what they mean. And to be intelligent, you have to use knowledge and information in original, creative ways. None of the current generation of robots can do this.

---

* For more about computer AI (artificial intelligence), see 'Will computers ever be smarter than people?' in the last chapter of *Why Is Snot Green?*

Will robots ever become intelligent?

Almost certainly, yes.

When?

Experts reckon that at the current rate of development, the first truly intelligent robots – nimble, agile robots with true **artificial intelligence** – will probably arrive within the latter half of this century (i.e. some time after 2050). Already, engineers are making small steps toward this. The **XPERO** robot, built by a group of European universities working together,

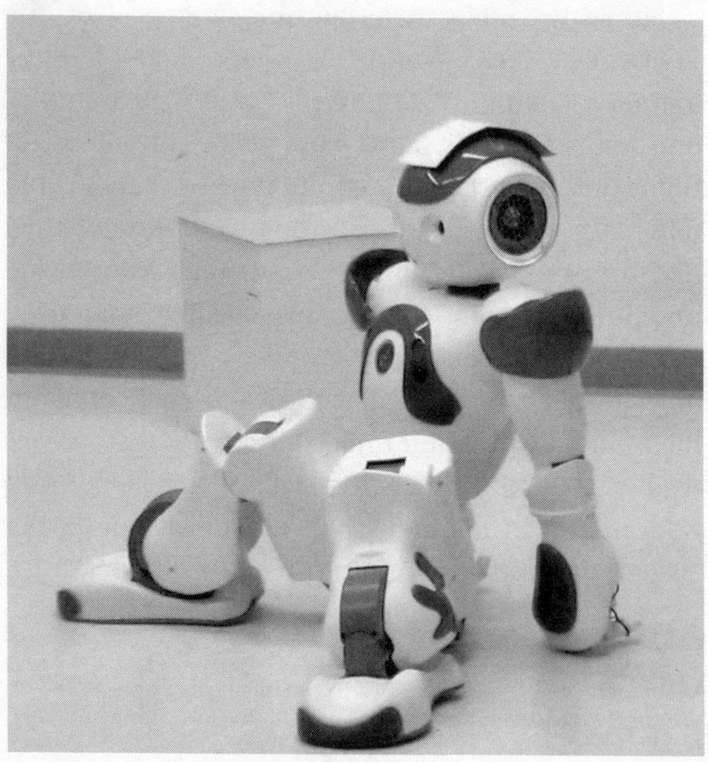

can learn about its own movement and environment by observing and experimenting, much as human babies and toddlers do. Meanwhile, the child-like CB2 robot – built by Japanese engineers at Osaka University – not only looks like a human toddler (complete with human-like eyes, eyelids, lips, ears and skin), it learns to interact with people by watching their facial expressions, just as a human baby would.

That sounds kind of creepy. Not sure I'd want some freaky robot watching me all day long.
Better get used to it. The 'smartbots' aren't here yet, but they're coming . . .

How small is the world's tiniest robot, and how big is the biggest?

The smallest is so tiny that you could fit a million of them inside a blood cell. The largest is a 12-metre-tall transforming robot dinosaur that breathes fire, crushes cars and eats aeroplanes. How cool is that?

Oh, okay. Wait – what!? Are you serious, or are you just having me on?
I'm not kidding. It's true. Unless, of course, there have been smaller and larger robots builts since the last time I looked. Which is possible, I suppose . . .

But a million robots inside one blood cell? How could they make a robot that tiny?
In short, they built it out of self-assembling DNA molecules, rather than chunks of metal. The world's tiniest robot to date was built by a Chinese university research team in 2009, led by American chemistry professor Nadrian Seeman. They built it using strands of deoxyribonucleic acid (or DNA) – the same stuff found within the cells of all living creatures – folded up like bits of origami paper until they took the desired shape. The result was a two-armed **nanobot** measuring just 150 nanometres (or millionths of a millimetre) long, and 50 nanometres wide. This 'bot could then be used to place other chemical molecules together and build new sub-microscopic structures. A

bit like a crane on a construction site. Only about **50 billion** times smaller. As a grand finale, Dr Seeman then went on to create a pair of DNA 'robot legs', which scissor back and forth as if walking.

That's all very impressive and that, but those aren't *real* robots, are they?
What do you mean?

Well, they can't move around by themselves, respond to human commands, can they?
Not really, no. If that's what you're looking for, then you're probably talking about something around a thousand times larger. Engineers in Korea, Japan and elsewhere have built controllable **microbots** that look like tiny caterpillars. Designed to inch their way through blood vessels and other body tissues, some measure less than 500 micrometres (or half a millimetre) long. They're controlled by two, microscopic **actuators** that allow them to follow one of two commands ('move forward', or 'turn'), and are powered by tiny electrical currents they absorb from surfaces around them.

If you're looking for something a little more fun, within the last few years, engineers and robot hobbyists have built other microbots like the **PicoBot** and **Echo-B**. These look like little metallic cubes on wheels, and stand just 25 mm (or 1 inch) tall. The Picobot zips around on its 3-mm-wide wheels, sensing

and avoiding obstacles in its path. The Echo-B goes one better – whole teams of them can be pitched against each other in miniature football matches.

Okay, that's pretty cool. But what about walking, talking robots? How small do they get?

As of 2010, the smallest humanoid robot (or robot that moves in a humanlike way) is probably the Tomy **i-Sobot**. This entertainment (or toy) robot stands around 16 cm (6.5 inches) tall and responds to a range of human commands. The i-Sobot walks, talks, dances, waves, does push-ups, somersaults and more. At present, an i-Sobot costs over £200 – which is roughly one pound per centimetre in height. But as the technology improves, then toy robots like this

will probably become smaller (and cheaper) still. Fancy a pet robo-bug? They're probably not far off.

All right, then. So that's the tiniest. What about the other end of the robo-scale? How big do the big-uns get?

Most of the world's biggest and strongest robots are industrial robots, used in factories. Among the mightiest of these are the **Fanuc m-2000** and the **Kuka TITAN**. These are both heavy-duty 'handling 'bots' – huge, robotic arms with powerful claws and grippers. They stand up to 3 metres (10 feet) tall, weigh up to 5,000 kg (5 tonnes) and can lift loads of up to

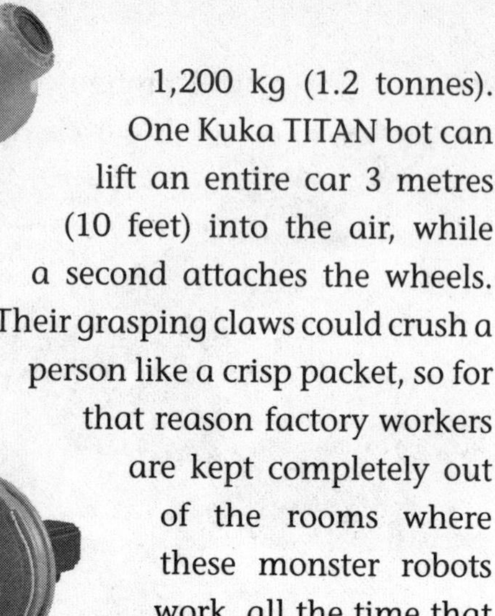

1,200 kg (1.2 tonnes). One Kuka TITAN bot can lift an entire car 3 metres (10 feet) into the air, while a second attaches the wheels. Their grasping claws could crush a person like a crisp packet, so for that reason factory workers are kept completely out of the rooms where these monster robots work, all the time that they are working.

Whoa. They sound pretty scary. Are they the biggest, then?

Not quite. The biggest, scariest robot built to date is probably **Robosaurus** – a 12-metre (40-foot) tall transforming robot dinosaur.

A transforming robot dinosaur?? What on Earth does that do?

For the most part, it burns and eats cars, trucks and small aeroplanes at American 'monster truck' rallies. Robosaurus was built in 1989, by American inventor (and *Transformers* fan) Doug Malewicki. 'Robo' as he calls it, can crush cars and planes with its massive claws and jaws, and breathe fire through flamethrowers set into each nostril. When in use, the operator (or pilot) sits in the head of this metallic beast and controls the claws, jaws and flamethrowers from there. When not in use, Robosaurus can transform itself into a box-shaped lorry trailer for towing around on roads.

That . . . is . . . awesome. Can I have one?

If you have a spare $575,000 (roughly £350,000) lying around, then yes. Or you could build your own, I suppose. In any case, good luck convincing your parents to let you keep it . . .

How many robots are there in the world?

It's hard to know for sure, but there are probably over ***nine million*** *working robots on the planet. If you know where to look, you can find them in factories, farms, power plants and mines all over the world, and in many places they're even invading our schools and homes! Robots do a huge range of different jobs for us – most of which humans could not (or would rather not) do for themselves. So it's perhaps not surprising that the robots are on the rise.*

Nine million? That's a lot of robots! That's, like, an entire city full of them!

That's right, it is. And although these nine million robots don't (of course) all live in the same place, if they did, there would be enough of them to fill New York or London. Put another way, the world's current robot population is bigger than the human population of Scotland or Sweden, and more than *twice* that of Ireland or Israel. So, if they wanted to, the robots could happily fill a whole *country*.

Whoa. But what would they call it?
'Robot-o-stan', maybe? 'The Robot Republic?'
How about 'Robo-nesia'?

Nice!
Thank you. I try.

So what are all those robots up to? I mean, how many jobs can a robot really do?

They're up to all sorts of things, and they do more jobs than you can possibly imagine. Engineers often classify robots into three main types or groups: **industrial robots, professional robots** and **personal** (or **service**) **robots**.

Industrial and professional robots come in a wide range of different shapes and sizes. They typically do jobs that are considered too **dull, dirty** or **dangerous** for human workers. Robot engineers call these sorts of tasks 'the three Ds'. And believe me, there are a lot of them.

Like what?

Well, you could argue that lots of jobs are **dull**. Since the Industrial Revolution, factory workers around the globe have found themselves parked in front of conveyor belts – filling bottles, assembling toys and gadgets, or packing finished products into boxes for shipping and selling. It's not that humans *can't* do these jobs. But it is impossibly boring to do these same tasks hour after hour, day after day, year in, year out. Humans can only work so fast, and so hard, before they drop. And they can't work too long without stopping to rest, eat, drink, pee, sleep and go home to see their families.

Not so for robots. Factory robots can fill hundreds of milk cartons, or bottle millions of aspirin pills in a single hour. And they do it, non-stop, for years. What's more, advanced industrial and professional robots can do jobs with a precision humans just can't match. So, in addition to all the robot stackers, packers and assemblers, there are also robots that milk cows, robots that defuse bombs* and robots that perform brain surgery.

What about the dirty and dangerous jobs?

Again, there are lots of those in the world. As the old saying goes, 'It's a dirty job, but somebody's gotta do it'. But given the choice, most people would rather not. And as robots become more flexible, mobile and agile, more and more of the truly **dirty** jobs are being handed over to our metallic friends. So there are wriggling robotic 'worms' which shuffle through pipes clogged with sewage, and there are robot 'moles' that dig and drill all day in mines choked with coal dust.

* For more about these, see 'Will future wars be fought by robots?' on page 212.

Where the dirty jobs end, the truly **dangerous** ones are just beginning. Many work environments – like mines, forges, oil rigs and nuclear reactors – are dangerous enough to claim thousands of human lives in industrial accidents every year. But thankfully, once again, it's robots to the rescue.

In most car assembly plants, it's now robots that do most of the heavy lifting. A single, multi-million-pound 'manipulator' 'bot can pick up a door, roof or exhaust pipe stacked on a shelf behind it, lift it into place and weld it to the growing body of a car in a matter of seconds. Deep beneath the sea, underwater 'bots are used to salvage shipwrecks or repair the legs of an oil-rig platform, at depths and pressures that would crush human divers. And in nuclear power plants robots work right in the heart of the hot, radioactive reactor core – lifting and lowering the fuel rods to keep powerful nuclear reactions under control.

Whoa. That's at least one job *I* wouldn't fancy.

Me, neither. And these are just a few of the reasons why more and more industrial and professional robots are being built each year.

What about the other ones? What did you call 'em – the *personal* robots?

Yep – they're on the rise, too. Personal service robots include everything from robot vacuum cleaners and lawnmowers to robot toys, pets, learning 'bots and

hobby 'bots. Almost a million Roombas (a popular robot vacuum cleaner) were sold in 2008 alone, and with floor sweeping and mopping versions joining the party, soon millions of homes could have robot cleaners trundling around their floors. In the last decade, toy robots like Pleo, RoboRaptor and RoboSapien have become playpals for thousands of kids around the world, and the new generation of toy robots and pets* – with advanced AI and speech recognition – will leave those early efforts in the dust. Meanwhile, Japan and South Korea are working feverishly on educational 'learning 'bots' for schools, and thousands of robot hobbyists are designing, building and battling their own DIY robots in their own homes.

* Read more about robot pets in 'Do geeks keep robot pets?' on page 204.

Wow. It sounds like *everyone* will own a robot before long. So will they?

Probably not *everyone*, no. As popular as robots are becoming, getting people to *buy* robots depends on how cheaply engineers can build them, and how wealthy each household is. Right now, the cost of batteries and motors is holding robot development back as it makes home robots too expensive for most people to afford.

Boo.

Even so, around 2 million more robots are being built and sold each year. So at the current rate there will be **almost a billion** robots on the planet by 2050, and **almost 2 billion** by the end of the century. That's nearly a third of the human population of the world. And who knows – once new power sources and technologies become available, there could be far more.

Like, the robots could outnumber the people?

Yup. Could be.

That's a little scary.

Let's just hope they keep doing what they're told. Otherwise you'll be battling Roombas and RoboRaptors all day long . . .

Do geeks keep robot pets?

Some of them do, yes! There are a wide range of robotic animals out there, including robo-cats, robo-dogs, robo-snakes, robo-mice and scuttling robo-cockroaches. But it's not just geeks that keep them, and they're not all created to be pets. Besides entertainment, robotic animals are also used for healing, spying and saving human lives.

Really? There are real-life robo-dogs? You can buy them?

Yep. In fact, they've been around for quite a while. Sony's **AIBO** robotic dog has been around since the 1990s, and over 150,000 people have bought and adopted one. AIBO can walk, play and perform common doggie tricks like 'sit', 'stay' and 'roll over' (plus a few *less* common ones, like 'dance', 'handstand' and 'somersault'!). Its specially designed software allows it to mature from a clumsy, curious pup into an adult dog that understands a hundred or more commands, and later versions could even take pictures with its digital camera 'eyes' and send them to your computer via a Wi-Fi connection. Although Sony stopped making them in 2006, devoted AIBO owners still hold annual AIBO 'dog shows', and until recently, whole teams of AIBOs would compete in the four-legged robot soccer tournament known as the **RoboCup**.

They stopped making them? But they sound brilliant!

Yes, they did. Fun as they were, AIBOs were expensive to build, so couldn't be sold cheaply enough for most people to afford (a brand-new AIBO cost between £1,000 and £2,000!) But the good news is Sony say they'll be using the AIBO technology in their next generation of robo-pets, which will (hopefully) be much cheaper when they finally arrive in the shops.

Sweeeeet. What about robo-cats?

Yep – they exist, too. Although (perhaps just like real cats) they aren't nearly as active or willing to perform tricks as AIBO. The Japanese toy company Sega already sells the **Yu-me Neko** ('Dream Cat') – a

fluffy robotic moggy covered with soft artificial fur, and equipped with a wide array of touch sensors that help it react just like a real (if somewhat lazy) kitty. Yu-me Neko doesn't walk or dance like AIBO. If you're lucky, it'll sit up for a bit, but for the most part it just lies there, waiting for you to stroke it. When petted, it closes it eyes, purrs and even rolls on its back for a belly rub. If you tug its tail, it yowls and hisses. When left alone for a bit, it'll miaow for attention, wash its face with a fuzzy paw or just curl up in a ball and go to sleep. So pretty much the same as a real cat.*

* Except, perhaps, for the 10% of the day that a real cat spends NOT resting, and doing other things like eating, swatting at laser pointers and flicking cat litter all over the floor. At least, that's what mine do.

One of the most advanced robo-pets to date is **Pleo** – a robotic baby dinosaur that learns from his environment using a complex microprocessor and over 38 sensors to detect light, motion, touch and sound. Once charged up and set free, Pleo will set about exploring your bedroom – avoiding obstacles or nudging them around with his nose to see if they're movable. If you tap him on the shoulder, he'll turn his head to look at you. If he hears a noise, he'll stroll towards it and investigate. And, if you introduce one Pleo to another, they recognize and talk to each other via nose-mounted infrared communication modules. (But be careful, because they can also catch colds from each other.)

Wow! He sounds pretty excellent. One thing, though . . .

What's that?

If you're going to go to all that trouble to buy a robot pet that acts *almost* like the real thing, then why not just buy a *real* pet instead?

Good point. Well, apart from the fact that you can't buy a *real* baby dinosaur (not yet, anyway), real animals take a lot more looking after. Real cats and dogs need to be fed, walked, taken to the vet, cleaned up after and boarded when you go away on holiday. But an AIBO doesn't require 'walkies' or a dog-sitter. And you'll never have to shovel a Yu-me Neko's filthy litter box.

Hmmm. I didn't think of that.

Besides that, not everyone *can* own a pet. Some people are allergic to dog or cat hair, while others live in places where animals are not allowed. One really great use found for robot pets is in comforting hospital patients (especially children) whose illnesses mean that they have to stay in hospitals for weeks, months or years. Medical studies have revealed that pet owners often recover from illness more quickly than people without pets, as having a loving cat or dog around can help reduce stress, and keep your spirits up. Unfortunately, *real* animals aren't allowed on most hospital wards, as they have to be kept very clean to prevent the spread of bacteria. But with a robo-pet even the very ill can enjoy having a faithful or fuzzy pal, and get many of the benefits of keeping a real animal.

Okay – so that explains the robo-cats and robo-dogs. But who in their right mind would ever want a robo-snake or robo-cockroach? Yuck. The real ones are gross enough.

Ah, but those aren't really built to keep as pets. They're made for quite different jobs.

Robotic snakes are currently being tested in North and South America for use in search and rescue operations, like sifting through rubble to find survivors after an earthquake. **The Omnitread Serpentine robot**, for example, is a 1.2-metre (4-foot) robotic snake that can crawl over any type of terrain, slither into holes just 10 cm (4 inches) wide and tunnel beneath heavy bricks or boulders to find people trapped beneath. Meanwhile, on the other side of the world, the Israeli army is testing a 2-metre (6-foot), camouflaged robot snake equipped with a digital camera, which wriggles through undergrowth to sneak up and spy on enemy positions.

A sneaky, snaky spy-bot?

Exactly. Spy-bots are of huge interest to military engineers, so it's often the military that pay for research into robotic animals (some of which then end up as toys or pets!). That's also the reason for building robotic cockroaches, bees and beetles. Robotics experts have already built robo-roaches that can scuttle into pitch-black rooms, feel their way around walls and obstacles with robotic antennae and take infrared or thermal pictures with on-board cameras. So far, they're way too big and slow to be of much use, but it probably won't be long before new technologies allow them to be built smaller, faster and smarter.

The *real* goal for future robo-animal-spies, though, is a robot bee or beetle, which can fly unseen into secret areas, snapping pictures and gathering information as it goes. So far, building **micro aerial vehicles** (or **MAVs**) like this has proved very difficult, since it's much harder to achieve controlled flight with tiny robots like this than it is with larger robot aeroplanes and helicopters.* But, again, it probably won't be too long before engineers figure it out.

Seriously?

Yep. In fact, one team of researchers has even tried attaching computer chips and cameras, and

---

* For more on these, see 'Will future wars be fought by robots?' on page 212.

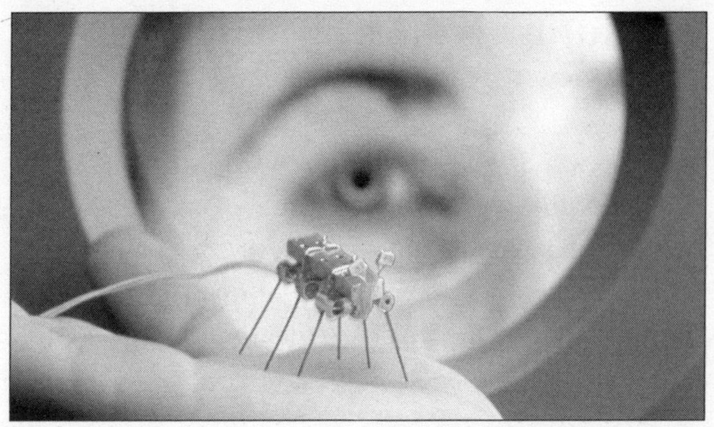

electrodes, to *real* beetles, creating freaky 'cyborg bugs' that can be steered towards targets by human controllers. What's more, it actually *worked.* By sending signals from a computer chip stuck to the beetle's back to wires embedded in the beetle's brain and wing muscles, engineers successfully steered a beetle through an obstacle course with several left and right turns, and got it to stop and land.

***Cyborg spy-beetles*? Okay, now I'm *officially* freaked out. I mean – they could be watching us *right now* . . .**
Wait – is that one, there? Quick, hide!

What?! Where?
My mistake. It was just a regular bug. Heheheheh.

Grrrrrrr. You'd better hope I don't set my AIBO on you.

Will future battles be fought by robots?

Yes, they will. In fact, robot drones have ***already*** *helped to fight battles in several war-torn regions of the world. Like it or not, robots are already part of many modern armies, navies and air forces. Right now, their numbers are small. But by the look of it, the world's robot fighting forces will only get bigger in the future.*

Seriously?! Robots are actually out fighting wars, right now? Where?

Right now, there are robot drones on patrols and missions in various parts of the Middle East and Asia. Most of these are owned and operated by the United States, the United Kingdom and Israel. But word has it that over forty countries across the globe are either operating or building their own military robots.

What do they look like?

That depends on the job they have to do. The most common ones are **unmanned aerial vehicles** (or **UAVs**), which fly airborne scouting, spying or attack missions. They look like small, grey, 'toy' aircraft – much like the aeroplanes and helicopters built by radio-controlled (or RC) model aircraft enthusiasts. (This is really no coincidence, as many modern military drones were actually based on RC hobby aircraft designs.)

Some, like the **MQ-8 Fire Scout**, look like full-size helicopters, only with no see-through cockpit or windows. But most look like small gliders or aeroplanes with wingspans ranging from 1 metre to 20 metres (3 to 60 feet) across. The **RQ-11 Raven** drone, for example, measures just 130 cm (55 inches) across, and weighs less than 2 kg (4 lb). But it can fly over 10 km (6 miles) on a single scouting mission, at speeds of up to 60 mph (100 kph). Ravens are mostly used to take pictures of enemy camps and targets, using their on-board digital or infrared cameras. But at the other end of the scale the fearsome **MQ-9 Predator** combat drone is a full-size aeroplane with a 20-metre (66-foot) wingspan, weighing over 2 tonnes (5,000 lb) even before it's loaded with laser-guided bombs and missiles.

So these robot aircraft actually, like, shoot people and bomb people?
Some of them do, yes. Although, technically, it's the human controllers or pilots who are doing the shooting and bombing – the robot drone is just the tool or weapon that allows them to do it. For now, at least, there are no robots battling without human control.

Once launched, a whole squadron of Predators can be flown remotely by pilots thousands of miles from where the war is actually going on. In fact, many UAVs currently in use in the Middle East are being flown by pilots at air force bases in Nevada or New Mexico, in the south-western USA. But while some robot drones are used for air attacks most are simply used for spying and scouting the battlefield. And besides UAVs there are lots of other military robots out there, too – doing lots of other jobs.

Like what?
On the ground, bomb disposal robots have been used for decades in war zones to remove landmines, car-bombs and other explosive booby-traps. And in the last few years a whole new class of **unmanned ground vehicles** (**UGVs**) sporting legs, wheels or tank-tracks have been scuttling and rolling their way into military operations. There are UGVs that look like miniature tanks, which roll into houses to look for lurking enemies. There are UGVs that look like

oversized beetles, which scuttle up walls and peer into windows with their camera-laden antennae. And there are UGVs like large, headless dogs, designed to trot and leap into firefights carrying weapons and ammunition for troops!

For the most part, this is how many military experts see robots being used in the future – more like helpful robot dogs than deadly 'battle-droids' or 'Terminators'. The Boston Dynamic 'Big Dog' behaves literally like a helpful dog. It has four dog-like legs that allow it to walk, trot and leap over obstacles that would be tricky for wheels or tank-tracks to roll over.

US Army engineers are already imagining a future combat system (or FCS) for their troops, in which each soldier is accompanied by a whole pack of up to twelve helpful 'bots – ranging from hovering robot scouts and spotters to trundling or trotting robot 'packbots' (like the Big Dog) laden with gear.

Why are fighting robots so popular?

Well, as we've already said, robots are handy for the 'three Ds' – things so dull, dirty or dangerous that no human really wants to do them. And one thing's for certain: while war may not be dull, it's certainly a dirty, dangerous business.

From an army commander's point of view, robots are pretty marvellous. For starters, there's no need to recruit or train robot soldiers – you just build them, and they're yours. And once you have your robot troops there's no need to pay them, feed them, or keep them happy. A robot never gets hungry, never gets stressed or depressed. And it will work or fight for years without rest, through freezing winter nights or endless days in the blazing desert sun. Perhaps best of all, no one really cares when a robot is damaged or destroyed. It's either rebuilt, or forgotten about. But there are no hospital bills to pay, no funerals to attend and no human families left behind to mourn the loss. Looked at this way, you could argue that replacing human troops with robots saves lives – as fewer human soldiers, sailors and pilots are put at risk.

But isn't battling with robots a bit – you know – risky? I mean, what if one of them made a mistake and bombed the wrong house? Or went crazy and shot an innocent person?

Well, some people would argue that this happens to *human* pilots and soldiers, too. In fact, some might say that robots are *more reliable* than people, as they have no fear or anger, and are less likely to make mistakes in the heat of battle. Combat robots are also built with special 'failsafe' mechanisms, so that they can't arm their weapons or fire upon targets without a human giving the command (or 'pulling the trigger'). So as long as humans are always in control, making the final life-or-death decisions, then we shouldn't have to worry about rogue 'Terminators' flipping

out and shooting people by themselves.

Others might argue that getting robots to do our dirty work makes it more likely that we'll wage wars, resulting in more deaths, not less. After all, if you're thousands of miles away from where the battle is raging – shooting and bombing via remote control – then waging war could feel more like a videogame than the real thing. Only it's not a game, because real people are getting hurt.

But what if it was all just robots-versus-robots? What if robot armies just fought our battles for us, with no human soldiers or victims involved?
Good question. You could say that this would be the best kind of battle, since no human lives need be lost. But if you think about it, eventually, one side would lose (i.e. run out of working robots) and start to advance. Then it wouldn't be long before they encountered real people, and it was robots-versus-people once more. Now instead of facing an army of living, breathing human soldiers, the 'losers' would be facing a horde of battle-hardened robots, all trundling, buzzing and swarming their way into town. I wouldn't want to face that, would you?

I'd rather not face either, thank you very much. Can't we just avoid wars altogether, and find a way to get along instead?
Well, that's not up to the robots – that's up to us . . .

Are some people really robots in disguise?

Sadly, no. At least, not unless you're reading this book some time after the year 2050. Right now, we simply don't have the technology to create humanoid robots (or androids) that look and act 'human' enough to fool us. And although some pretty impressive androids have already been built experts reckon it'll be a long while before truly humanlike robots walk among us, unnoticed.

So we can build androids, just not ones that can fool us into thinking they're human?
Exactly.

Why not? I mean, they make those waxwork models of celebrities that look real enough, right? So why not real-looking androids?
Because sculpting a waxwork model is much, much simpler than building a walking, talking android. For a waxwork to look real, it just has to stand there. For an android to look real, it not only has to look like a person, it also has to move, talk and act like a person, too. A realistic waxwork can fool you at first glance, but since it then fails to move or do anything, we realize it's not real within seconds. Similarly, the current generation of androids (or at least some of them) can look real enough at first glance, and when they start to move and speak they may even fool

you into thinking they're human for an extra second or two. But so far no one has managed to build an android that looks human, walks and moves like a human, and reacts to people and speech in truly realistic, human ways.

That's partly because we human beings are hugely complex and sophisticated creatures. Our bodies contain over 200 movable joints, joined together by over 600 separate muscles. Moving them in different directions and combinations gives us over 1,300 possible movements (engineers would say we have over 1,300 possible **degrees of freedom**). Our facial expressions (like smiles, frowns and grimaces of disgust) are controlled by over 30 separate muscles. Today's androids don't have anywhere near as many joints, motors and artificial 'muscles', and none has more than 100 degrees of freedom. So, for all their complex designs and structures, their movements and facial expressions still look stiff, wooden and 'robot-like', rather than convincingly human or 'life-like'.

So how good are today's androids, and where can you find them?

Some of them are pretty good (far from perfect, but convincing enough to make you look twice!). The most advanced androids are currently being built in Korea and Japan.

Like that ASIMO robot you talked about before?

Not so much him, no. While ASIMO was created to mimic human movements (specifically, walking movements), he wasn't really built to look human. He's a humanoid robot, but he's not really an android. If you covered ASIMO with skin, he still wouldn't look human – he's square-edged, stocky and has no human facial features at all. But other Japanese and Korean androids do look human.

In 2003, Japanese engineers from Osaka University revealed their doll-like female **Actroid** robot at the International Robot Exhibition in Tokyo. The original Actroid had human-like body proportions, hair and facial features, but could not stand up, and could only move its arms and facial 'muscles' in very limited ways. But two years later, the designers unveiled their new, improved Actroid – called **Repliee Q1** – at the 2005 World's Fair in Nagoya. This Actroid had realistic silicon skin, and ten more degrees of freedom (DOF) in its movement than the original model, making its facial features and hand gestures much more realistic. Later, the same team went on to build the Dramatic Entertainment Robots **DER-01** and **DER-02** – free-standing (and attractive-looking) female androids designed to meet and greet people with realistic human gestures and speech. When **DER-03** was finally revealed in 2008, she had such realistic features and movements that she fooled (and even frightened) many reporters.

Korea's answer to the Actroid was the **Eve-R1** education and entertainment android. Unveiled in 2003, she was built by a team at the Korean Institute of Industrial Technology, and looked very much like Repliee Q1 – a seated, female android with realistic facial expressions (like fear, surprise and anger) and arm gestures. In 2005, the same team followed up with **Eve-R2**, a free-standing female android with enhanced facial expressions (including boredom and irritation) which could chat with children in a classroom, or mime along with pre-recorded songs on stage. A later model, Eve-R3, performed an entire musical stage play alongside human actors in 2010, playing the lead role in *Snow White and the Seven Dwarfs*!

As of 2010, 'Fembots' – based on the Actroid DER-03 – have been available to buy in Japan. For the tidy sum of 20 million Yen (around £150,000), one of these realistic female androids could be sitting on your sofa – singing songs, giggling at your jokes and more. But don't expect her to cook you dinner, or head out with you to meet your friends. The Fembot cannot move at all from the waist down.

That's not much good, is it? An android that just sits or stands there is kind of boring. How long before they make one that walks and moves like a real person?

Well, in 2009, Japan's National Institute of Advanced Industrial Science and Technology (AIST) revealed a walking, talking, singing, '**girlbot**' with a range of realistic human walking movements, dance movements and facial expressions. She can strut down a catwalk like a fashion model, sing (or rather lip-sync) to a variety of pre-programmed songs and perform simple dance choreographies alongside real human dancers.

The girlbot, or **HRP-4C** as she's officially known, was designed more for stage entertainment than interacting with people. Her realistic skin, hair and other human-like features only extend to her face, head, neck and hands – the rest of her body is more or less the right shape, but is covered with metal and plastic body-armour that makes her look like a *Star Wars* stormtrooper. And her fairly primitive computer 'brain' makes her little more conversational than your average toaster or microwave. But she's probably the most realistic-looking android* to date, and she's certainly a step in the direction of creating truly humanlike robots.

---

* The correct term for a female humanlike robot is actually **gynoid**, rather than android. Best remember that for the future, if you don't want to offend your robot girlfriends . . .

Perhaps the most frighteningly realistic androids built so far are the Geminoid robots built by Japanese robotics professor Hiroshi Ishiguro. Geminoids are androids built to look exactly like their masters or creators, and Professor Ishiguro has built one modelled on himself (Geminoid HI), on a Japanese model friend (Geminoid F) and Danish Robotics professor Henrik Scharfe (Geminoid DK). While none of these can walk or talk like their masters, they look real enough at first glance to fool many people.

It'll probably be another fifty or sixty years, at least, before we can build androids that can not only look human, but can also understand natural human speech, understand the things they see with their digital eyes and understand human actions, motivations and emotional states.

One of the toughest goals of robotics and artificial-intelligence research is to build a computer (or robot brain) that can pass the Turing Test – first devised by mathematician Alan Turing over forty years ago. In the Turing Test, a human test subject is placed in front of a computer screen and chats – usually in typed text – with an onscreen partner. In one part of the test, the unseen partner is another, real, human on another computer. In a different part of the test, it's a computer or robot partner using its artificial intelligence and language programs to try and sound human.

So far, no computer has managed to fool a human subject into thinking it was really a person (at least not for more than a minute or so). When a computer or robot does pass the Turing Test, we'll be a lot closer to building truly intelligent robots, which might realistically pass for human beings.

Once that happens, could androids start to replace people?

In some ways, yes – they could. In today's world, we already see that many jobs and tasks tend to flow towards wherever they can be done most cheaply. That's why many European banks hire people in Asia to answer customer phone calls, because it's so much cheaper than paying European workers, while many American and Canadian businesses build their factories in South America for similar reasons.

There will almost certainly come a time – probably sometime in the latter half of this century – when buying and running a robot will be cheaper than paying a human worker to do the same job, for the same length of time. When that happens, robots will start to pop up everywhere, replacing human workers in the more boring, menial jobs like sitting at roadside toll booths, or giving directions and information at train stations, airports and shopping centres. And, as robots become more advanced, the number of jobs they can do will become greater and greater.

But what if they decide to replace us altogether? Like, wage war, start building themselves, disguise themselves as us and take over the world?

Not likely. For starters, they'll still have human programmers, who will build in safety circuits and programming rules* that prevent them from harming people, and force them to obey human commands, no matter what.

But what if those circuits got busted, or the programming went wrong?

Well, then we'd have a problem.

I guess we'd better be nice to our robots. You know – just in case . . .

---

* For more about these, including the three Laws of Robotics, see 'Will evil computers and robots take over the world?' in *Why Is Snot Green?*

Answers

Activity: Computer Bits and Pieces solution from page 23

page 23

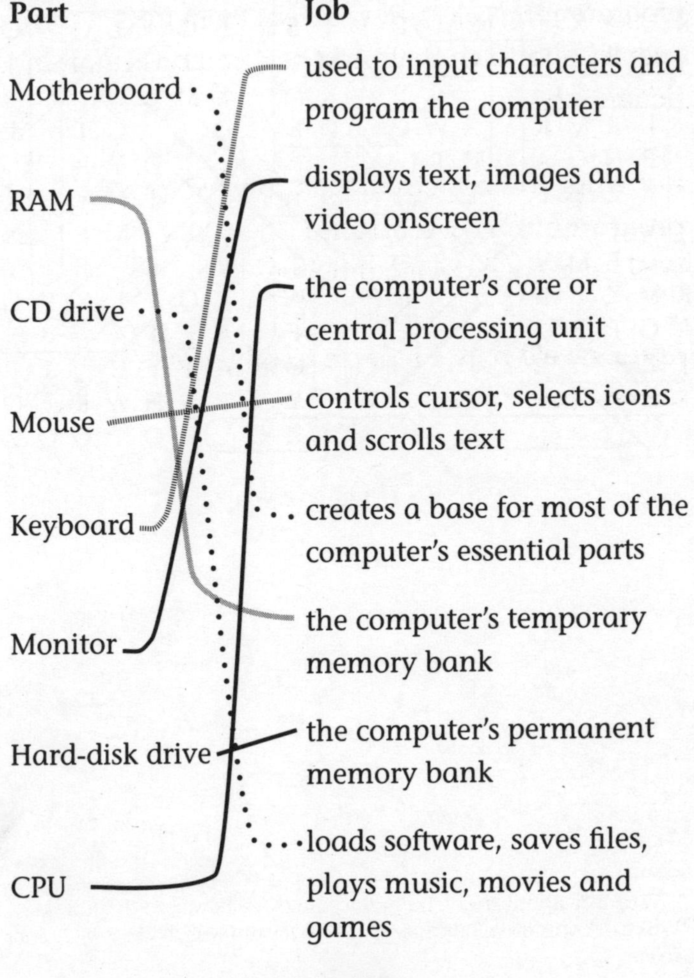

Geekspeak solution from page 36

1(a). 2(c). 3(b). 4(a). 5(c).

Police Codes Puzzle solution from page 78/79

T U K M U U O F V M R R C H A R L I E T
K U A X Z U L U D I T S E E G A L Q N O
E M B Z D N O X V Z M G B I I G T N O J
A P A P S I E R R A K M E X M E H L V S
L L R M K F X W O O D N U D R O G I E F
P E N G A O H R E C H O O O T D Y R M D
H A Z K E R L M O G N A T E S T N Y B K
A V J R B M O A B A H C L O E C M L E X
S U E M V R I J D D I J I V R Z A P R V
R M X Z K K A K N V N W M L Q T L R V G
A G F R G U I V E Y D F A A E T X R A Y
J Z F O X Z J L O O I Q N A T Y U O T P
J U L I E T Z Y O W A Y V P A H W R F Q
K F W H I S K Y Y A N K E E E Q I G Q Z

Puzzle: Music and Movies Crossword solution from page 124.

		1 L	I	G	2 H	T	Y	E	A	R
	3 C				A					
	O			4 E	R	E	A	D	E	5 R
	M				R					E
	P				Y		6 I			C
7 H	A	R	D		P		N			O
	C				O		F			R
	8 T	O	Y	S	T	O	R	Y		D
					T		A			
					E		R			
9 A	10 V	A	T	A	R		E			
	I						D			
11 E	D	I	S	O	N					
	E									
12 W	O	O	D	Y						

Internet Word Search solution from page 156

Question from page 165

Q Who ruled Egypt from 2589 to 2566 BC?

A Khufu, better known as Cheops.

Quick Email Quiz solution from page 177

1(c). 2(c) 3(b). 4(a). 5(c).

Picture credits

The Publisher would like to thank the following for permission to reproduce their material. Every care has been taken to trace copyright holders. However, if there have been unintentional omissions or failure to trace copyright holders, we apologize and will, if informed, endeavour to make corrections in any future edition.

(Top = t; Bottom = b; Centre = c; Left = l; Right = r)

Illustrations by Mike Phillips, except:

Pages 10, 11, 16, 96, 108, 109, 110, 111, 112, 113, 129 Science Museum/Science and Society Picture Library; pages 27 Arturo Urquizo/Wikipedia; 28 Matarese-photos/Wikipedia; 81 European Space Agency; 84t Shutterstock/Israel Pabon; 84b Shutterstock/Manamana; 90t Shutterstock/Sergej Razvodovskij; 90b Shutterstock/Elnur; 115 Shutterstock/Natalia Siverina; 127 Getty/Hulton Archive; 131 Shutterstock/Levent Konuk; 136 Shutterstock/Monkey Business Images; 145 Getty/Hulton Archive; 153 01.camille/Wikipedia; 185 Shutterstock/DenisKlimov; 186 Getty/ Yoshikazu/AFP; 188 Getty/Tom Mihalek/AFP; 191 XPERO Project; 194 Cortical Café Wiki; 196 Kuka Robotics; 197 Shutterstock/Eugene Berman; 200 Institute of Neuroinformatics, Switzerland; 205 Freephotos.biz; 206 Getty/Yoshikazu/AFP; 207 Getty/Yoshikazu/AFP; 209 Mobile Robotics Lab, University of Michigan; 211 Science Photo Library/Peter Menzel; 213 Dammit/Wikipedia; 223 Getty/Yoshikazu/AFP; 224 Getty/Yoshikazu/AFP.

Index

SCIENCE SORTED

Space, black holes and stuff

Glenn Murphy

What is a black hole?

How do we know that stars and galaxies are billions of years old?

What is the difference between stars and planets?

Packed with information about all sorts of incredible things like supermassive black holes, galaxies, telescopes, planets, solar flares, constellations, eclipses and red dwarfs, this book has no boring bits!

SCIENCE SORTED

Evolution, nature and stuff

Glenn Murphy

How did we develop from chemical soup into internet-surfing human beings?

What is a selfish gene?

What are the kingdoms of life?

Evolution and genetics are like a map for exploring the whole world of living things. Trace the history of life right back to our earliest ancestors and you'll be amazed at what you find. This book tells you everything you need to know, with none of the boring bits!

SCIENCE SORTED

Brains, bodies, guts and stuff

Glenn Murphy

What happens in your head during a headache?
What are toes for?
Why are some farts eggier than others?

Glenn Murphy, author of *Why Is Snot Green?*, answers these and other brilliant questions in this hilarious and fascinating book about the human body.

This book explores everything from cells to organs, from breathing to blood-flow, from scabs and rashes to broken bones and brainpower. It's the human body with no boring bits!

Why is SNOT green?

The First Science Museum Question and Answer Book

Glenn Murphy

Why is snot green? Do rabbits fart? What is space made of? Where does all the water go at low tide? Can animals talk? What are scabs for? Will computers ever be cleverer than people?

Discover the answers to these and an awful lot of other brilliant questions frequently asked at the Science Museum in this wonderfully funny and informative book.

Stuff that scares your PANTS off!

The Science Museum Book of Scary Things (and ways to avoid them)

Glenn Murphy

What scares you most? Spiders or sharks? Ghosts or aliens? Dentists or darkness?

This amazing book takes apart your deepest, darkest fears. With a bit of biology, a spot of psychology and oodles of lovely facts and figures, you'll learn everything there is to know about the stuff that scares your pants off.